MAKING
Life Story
Books

Tony Ryan

Specialist Social Worker (Homefinding)
Leeds Social Services

Rodger Walker

Project Leader (Intermediate Treatment)
Barnardo's Yorkshire Division

*British Agencies for
Adoption & Fostering*

Acknowledgements

The notion of life story books has been around for a great many years. During our booklet's long gestation period, we have been exposed to numerous ideas, comments, suggestions and advice from colleagues, friends and foster/adoptive parents, as well as feedback from the seminars we have led and help from the children themselves. We are grateful to all of these, particularly to those who have given us permission to reproduce their work here.

There is no copyright on ideas but where we have been able to identify specific contributions we have done so. We particularly wish to express our gratitude for the help and support of colleagues at Barnardo's Yorkshire Division and at Leeds Social Services Department. For help with some of the photographs in this book we are indebted to John North. Finally we wish to thank our long-suffering wives, Margaret and Joy, for their tolerance, patience and encouragement.

Tony Ryan
Rodger Walker

British Agencies for Adoption & Fostering

11 Southwark Street, London SE1 1RQ

Copyright © BAAF 1985

ISBN 0 903534 60 6

Designed by Andrew Haig
Commissioned photography by Trefor Ball
and John North
Cover photography by Robert Duncan
Typeset by TNR Productions, London
Printed by Fulmar Colour Printing Co Ltd

Contents

Preface

Our introduction to 'life story book' work came from our involvement in finding new families for children who had become permanently separated from their birth parents. With improved training techniques for adopters and foster parents, we felt that our preparation of new families was reaching an acceptable level. It seemed to us that this was not so with our preparation of children for placement.

We had read books by Kay Donley and Claudia Jewett and had attended a BAAF meeting on ways of communicating with children using play, music and drama. Play techniques particularly appealed to us and we decided to learn some of these, thinking back particularly to Virginia Axline and her book *Dibs, in search of self*, published 20 years ago (and now available in Penguin Books). A further stimulus was provided by John Triseliotis and his book, *In Search of Origins* (Routledge and Kegan Paul 1973), particularly his references to the building of identity and to the needs of adopted people to know about their origins.

In time we drew all these threads together and set out to prepare our children for placement using the methods suggested. The publication of Vera Fahlberg's work (BAAF) came at just the time to encourage us that we were on the right lines.

We were amazed at the results we were able to achieve using life story books and at how positively the children responded to this approach. We began to discover what others had discovered before us: that helping children through their life story books is both rewarding and effective.

Gradually we gathered more and more information and we decided to write about what we were learning. This book is the result. We have tried to show how you can remove the mystery in a child's past and help that child to establish a positive sense of identity. Our ideas are not absolutes: they are ways that have worked for us. We hope they will help you to develop methods for working with which *you* feel comfortable.

When you are working on the life story book with your child, remember not to be afraid of the child's past: it cannot harm you. The only harm that it can do is when it is left alone in the hope that it will go away – then it can certainly harm the child. If the past is interfering with your child's present it will interfere with his or her future too, and with the future of *their* children. It is far better to bring the past into today, deal with it and slot it safely back where it belongs: understood, never forgotten, but safe.

4

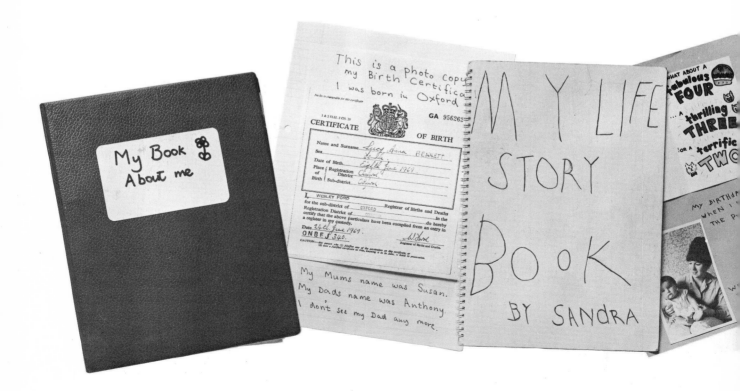

What is a life story book?

A life story book (or lifebook, as it is sometimes called) is, as described by Vera Fahlberg, an account of a child's life in words, pictures, photographs and documents, made by the child with the help of a trusted adult.

Children who live with their birth families have the opportunity to know about their past and to clarify past events in terms of the present. Children in care are often denied this opportunity. They are separated from their birth families; they may have changed families, social workers, homes. Their past may be lost, much of it even forgotten.

When children lose track of their past, they may well find it difficult to develop emotionally and socially. If adults cannot or do not discuss this past with them, it is reasonable for children to suppose that it is very bad.

A life story book is an attempt to give back to the child in care his or her past life through the gathering and discussion of the facts and people in that life and to help him or her to accept it, and go forward into the future with this knowledge.

We have found that most children in care gain a great deal from talking about their past, present and future to a sympathetic adult. Making a life story book with a child is a way of giving a structure to this talk.[*]

Children in care, whether they are in a children's home, with a foster parent, going to a permanent new family or returning to their natural family, need to sort out why they are in care and why various adults have let them down. We have often failed in the past to do this for children for whom we have been responsible.

Our experience with children we have talked to through making life story books has encouraged us to believe that this is a useful way of fulfilling this need, and that all the children have benefitted in some way.

All children are entitled to an accurate knowledge of their past and their family. This is a right that children who are secure in their families take for granted. The right of children in care to this knowledge is important, not only for the sake of the children themselves, but also for their future children.

5

---

[*]Life story books have also been made by old people entering residential care to help give them a sense of worth about themselves and to help others appreciate them as whole people.

What do children get from making a life story book?

Making a life story book gives children a structured and understandable way of talking about themselves. It can produce clarity where there are dangerous fantasies. Once completed, it provides them with a record which they and, with their agreement, the adults caring for them can refer to at any time, particularly when there is a crisis.

Working towards a life story book can increase a child's sense of self-worth. It is a sad truth that at the back of the minds of nearly all children in care is the thought that they are worthless and unlovable. They blame themselves for the actions of adults. If they have been abandoned, neglected or injured by their parents or wider family, they are convinced that they brought it on themselves. A life story book gives you the opportunity to show them why they should be proud of themselves, and this positive attitude should run through the whole book. In talking about their natural parents, for example, although you will tell them a suitably-worded version of the truth (however painful that may be) about their family and why they are in care, it is important to stress the positive side. You need to talk about their natural parents in non-judgemental terms. Perhaps you might say that not everybody is good at being a parent, but that does not mean that they are bad in other respects.

When you have worked together on the book, you will feel much closer to the child. We ourselves have found that memories of our own childhoods are always awoken. If we, too, have experienced pain, we share this with the child – while always remembering whose story it is! Some people make life story books with more than one child at a time, and some sharing of experiences – without breaking confidences, of course – can make a child feel better. Thus a child can appreciate that many people experience pain in their childhood and that the fault does not lie with them: they need not feel guilt, as so many children, amazingly, do, for their parents' behaviour.

Finally, you need to be able to relax and enjoy at least some parts of each of the sessions and, for this, you may need to relearn how to play. This will give you a lot of fun! With some of the play techniques suggested later on, you will need to get down on the floor with the child and play with toys. Self-consciousness is not a virtue in this situation but, if you need a reason, you should know that your playing has a serious purpose and is a valuable technique of equal status to the ability to talk naturally to a child on important issues. While not every life story book will lead you into play, some will and you might as well enjoy yourself while you are playing!

About identity

A healthy sense of identity is vital to everybody. A poor sense of identity can disable children and adults alike, and limit their ability to take on fresh challenges, such as moving into a new family. At its worst a poor sense of identity can 'freeze' children so they have an over-investment in the past and cannot move on to think about the future. It can also cause apathy and a depressed, fatalistic outlook.

Identity is a complex concept; it probably starts in individuals with the first separation of 'inside' and 'outside' self at about six months. This creation of the idea of 'self' is crucial to healthy development and where it is hindered by events and by other people who are important (like mothers and fathers) not responding appropriately, severe problems can arise.

Whilst understanding 'self' is difficult, particularly for children severed from their roots and without a clear future, it is made easier by separating out some of the more easily definable parts and discussing them openly with a child. One way of doing this is to talk about the past, the present and the future.

The past is made up of places, significant dates and times, people, changes, losses or separations and other events, both happy and sad, like illnesses, holidays and birthdays.

The present is made up of self-images, reactions to the past and issues like What am I doing here? Where do I belong? How do others see me?

The future is made up of issues such as What shall I be? Where shall I live? What chances do I have? What other changes will there be?

In making a life story book with a child, all these things can be raised in ways that feel natural to a child. This will give you and the child opportunities to establish facts about the past and present and go some way towards demystifying events and people in the child's life. Similarly, hopes and doubts about the future can be raised and 'bridging' (linking the past to the future) into the new family or situation can begin.

6

This section on identity theory is necessarily brief and you may want to read more authoritative views. We have listed books for further reading at the end of this booklet.

Who should make life story books with children?

We firmly believe in the healing effect of talking. Any sympathetic adult who is prepared to spend the time and give the commitment to the child by making a life story book can be the right person to do it.

Anyone who takes on this task will need to enlist the active support of the child's social worker and others through regular discussions. We have successfully helped adoptive and foster parents and many residential social workers to work with children in this way.

What does making a life story book require of you?

Whoever makes the book with the child needs to have patience in order to pick up the child's clues, particularly during sessions when not a lot is happening because the child is not in the mood or is testing if you can be trusted. The person needs too to be sensitive to the child. There is no surefire way of making a life story book, but the child is always the key. It is your responsibility to find ways of letting your child tell you about his or her life, and avoid imposing your own views. Whilst you should not allow patently false information to go into the book, you also need to avoid taking over and writing the 'Authorised Version' of a child's life. It is the child's life story after all and it is how he or she views it that needs to be written down.

When you need to challenge a view or a fact, it should be done as a contribution to the discussion and not as a correction. You can disagree with a child without being overbearing or forcing your own view.

There are some mistakes which beginners sometimes make but which you should, with common sense, easily be able to avoid.

1. Never betray the child's confidences made to you.
2. Don't avoid talking about things the child wants to talk about because they make *you* uncomfortable.
3. Don't put words into the child's mouth.
4. Once you have taken on the making of a life story book, you must not abandon the child halfway through it and hope that someone else can complete your work. You should continue with it until both of you agree it is time to end your regular sessions on it.
5. Never use the making of the book as either a prize or a punishment, but only as a normal part of your life together.

When might you make a life story book?

A life story book can be started at any time when the adult and the child have enough confidence in each other to begin and the time to continue. Sometimes they are part of preparing a child who is going from a children's home to a family; sometimes they are made to help the child to accept life as it is.

Ideally, the decision to make a life story book will come at a review or case conference. At the same time it will be decided who does what and where. Everyone involved should then support the adult making the book, feeding them with facts and information and suggesting ways around problems. A foster or adoptive parent should look for support from their social worker and perhaps from other substitute parents, and have regular discussions about progress. Equally, if you are a social worker or residential social worker, good supervision is very important.

Other members of the 'team' involved with the child who hear of the child progressing or regressing, should tell the adult making the life story book about it. They should also be prepared to cope with the child reliving past experiences or looking for reassurance and possibly displaying disturbed behaviour. They need to understand that *this is all part of the healing process*.

Feedback to the 'team' is also a great help in making appropriate decisions about the child's future. However, it is important to repeat the warning about not betraying the child's confidences to *you*.

How do you deal with confidentiality?

The question of keeping confidential what a child tells you while you work together on a life story book is an important one, to which we have given much thought. Throughout the time we have worked with children we have tried to reach a satisfactory solution to the conflict between not betraying the child's trust and yet needing to share some of the information with others.

The difficulty is that the significant adults in the child's life, such as foster parents, social workers and residential social workers, may have a 'team' approach. They will feel that it is important to pool knowledge with the goal of helping their child. He or she, of course, will not regard this in the same way.

We have always found in our individual work with children that they desire that your discussions remain confidential to the two of you. Children may disclose something of the inner world which they are not prepared even to record in their life story book. For example, they may express anger against a person in their past. Yet this may have relevance for the future and you may feel it necessary to pass it on to others. In such circumstances, we would share the outline of the confidence only, without disclosing any details.

We always make it clear to the significant adults that their child will probably demand confidentiality about certain things and that we intend to respect this. It may be possible to explain to the child that you would like permission to talk to others about a particular disclosure because you believe it may help the child. You might be able to negotiate with the child what you are allowed to say. This in itself can be helpful to the child because it provides another format to discuss a possible painful event in the past. Only when the child has given us permission do we talk to others.

How does the life story book end?

There comes a stage when you *both* agree that you have reached the present day and covered everything you can, and that the regular sessions can end. This point is different for every child. However, you should be suspicious if the life story book has turned into little more than a photograph album and you are finished after only three or four sessions. In that situation, go back over the book and see if the child can write or draw about any particular period which you know (from the file or doing a questionnaire, as described later) to be sensitive.

We never regard the book as finished. It can be updated until adulthood. It can be turned to in a crisis, such as when a child revives a ghost or a myth from the past. Then you can go to the section of the book which dealt with it and gently rediscover the reality together.

We often find, for example, that when we discuss a new permanent family with a child, he or she will start to make up fantasies about the natural family, however badly they let them down. Children have a natural fear of letting go of their present relative security – however unsatisfactory that may be – to face a risky future. You can then look back together at the anger the child felt about the birth parents when doing the life story book. This may help him or her to let go more easily and face the future.

We have written this book as a result of our own experience with the intention of helping others who want to use life story books as a way of helping children. We hope that what we have said here will help and not discourage you. You may worry that you might damage a child or give him or her too much pain. If you are a person who has a commitment to the child, you are the right person to make the life story book and you will more than compensate in the long term for any pain the child might suffer in the short term. The only damage you can do is by walking away from your commitment before it is completed.

On my first visit to my new family.

2 Communicating with children

These 'Ten Commandments' from *Opening New Doors* by Kay Donley, former director of the Spaulding for Children Agency in New York, in our opinion 'says it all' when it comes to communicating with children.

1. Avoid clichés in talking to children.

Children recognise clichés and your use of them will readily and clearly inform the child that you are indeed an adult who does not know how to talk to them. Some of the typical cliches that adults use in working with children are questions, probing questions, such as, 'How do you like school? Which class are you in?' Never begin a conversation with a child in that way. Eventually, when you really know the child, such questions may be appropriate, but never as an opening gambit. The best way to begin a conversation with a child is simply to exchange some pleasantries about who you are and how pleased you are to know him and let it go for a while. Children are more responsive to the idea of approaching you gradually, than to being physically and psychically overwhelmed by this large thing that flies at them and begins to probe their inmost thoughts. Take your time. You never know at first if you have a very shy, withdrawn child or a very aggressive one.

2. Assume that any child you are going to work with has some deep concern that has never been adequately understood or answered.

I am referring specifically to children in public care, all of whom typically share the experience of having been separated from their parents. In many cases they have also lost a succession of care-takers – house parents and foster parents. In working with the child you may, in fact, discover that someone very skilled and very sensitive has helped him to understand what has happened. But it is safer to assume that no one has adequately assessed the deep and often confused concerns of the child.

3. Understand from the beginning that children in care have been hurt: some part of them has been damaged.

Never make the assumption that, because everyone presents this child as untouched and undamaged, he must be that way. More often than not, the child will have been handled by a lot of unperceptive people. Perhaps this particular child has made an exceptionally good adjustment in the face of difficult and painful circumstances. But as a rule, there are always some damaged pieces of unfinished business tucked away. If you understand that, you will not be dismayed or thrown off balance six months later when someone says: 'You know, there's something peculiar about this kid. He's not quite what I would call "normal".'

4. Remember that in working with a child your essential task is to learn how he explains himself to himself, and what he understands his situation to be.

Unless you really know what is going on inside him, you will not be able to represent him justly or truthfully to residential staff or to potential foster or adoptive parents. It is not simply that you must know where this child is for your own satisfaction. You must be prepared to communicate your understanding to other people. This is not easy.

5. Develop specific concrete tools which will help you communicate with children.

Children are not normally interested solely in verbalisation as a way of communicating with anyone. They have other available tools and you must find out what they are so that you can use them too.

6. Be prepared to become a dependable, predictable and regular fixture in the child's experience.

You simply cannot pop in on a Monday and say, 'I'll see you again sometime soon'. The social worker's indefinite promise of returning to his life usually means avoiding him for several weeks and then popping in again. This simply does not work and is, in fact, destructive. You are adding to the child's already increasing fund of knowledge that, as far as he is concerned, adults are undependable, unpredictable and unknowable. You must regularise your contact. Most social workers say, 'I really would like to, but I haven't the time'. This begs the question, because it is possible to regularise contacts, even if there are long intervals between visits. It is the idea of predictability that is important to the child. If you make a commitment then you keep it. (And I mean you keep it, even if it breaks your back!) If, for some reason, you are unable to keep the appointment you have made, it is important that you communicate directly with the child the reasons why you cannot. I have known workers go to the extent of sending a telegram to a child whom they could not reach by telephone, so strong was their sense of commitment.

7. Remember that each child's experience is unique and that it is absolutely crucial that each child is helped to begin to come to grips with his life.

You cannot begin on the assumption that, because you have worked successfully with one or two children who have been neglected by their parents, you know what this experience means to any child. Certainly, you can learn from one situation and apply

10

your knowledge to another. But keep in mind that you are dealing with individuals: deceptively similar experiences have very different meanings for different children.

8. As you work with a child over a period of time, you must help him develop what I call a 'cover story'.
'Cover story' is not a very good phrase because a lot of people think that I mean concealing things and I do not. I believe that a child must have a clear, understandable, acceptable explanation of his circumstances, which he must be able to use at will and comfortably. For example, when he goes to a new school, he will be meeting a lot of new children, making friends and meeting people living in the neighbourhood. He will be asked questions about himself and it is essential that he should have a socially acceptable and logical explanation for who he is and where he is and why he is in this situation. Only too frequently, unskilled workers do not appreciate how essential this is and do not help the child develop a 'cover story' for public consumption. Without it the child is left to his own devices and frequently falls into fabrication. A child fabricates when he is not quite sure how people will receive the true facts of his situation. Fabrication, once found out, will very quickly give the child a reputation in the neighbourhood for being a spinner of tall tales, or at worst, a liar.

9. Commit yourself always to what I call a multi-faceted or composite view of the child.
Remember there is no one true way of seeing and

experiencing a youngster. Every person who has contact with the child will have a slightly different point of view and a unique experience. Some people will be enthusiastic about him, while others cannot abide him. What you are really searching for is a combination for all those perceptions, because buried amongst all of them there is the truth. Somewhere, amongst all those varying views of the child, will be a perception that his potential adoptive parents may make of him. So it is important that you begin to develop that kind of sensitivity and awareness.

10. Keep in mind from the beginning of your work that you are obliged to convey to any care-takers – be they residential staff or adoptive families – a true sense of the child's history.
You may think that this is self-evident and that I am being needlessly repetitious in stressing this point. But I think it bears repeating, because many social workers feel they are doing a child a grave injustice by telling the full and sorry tale, and that the only way to spare the child is to conceal certain things. These are usually things the social worker finds distressing or unpalatable, so they are concealed because she feels that this will give the child a better chance in life, a better opportunity for placement, an easier adjustment. Invariably those very things come flashing up anew out of the child's history and past to create problems and difficulties for him and his caretakers. This is a painful area for most social workers but it is one which you must grapple with and come to terms with.

Before you begin

The idea of making a life story book should grow naturally if you talk and listen to what children say about their family and why they think they are in care. There are, however, guidelines which draw on Kay Donley's work as described in her 'Ten Commandments'.

1. The aim, both initially and throughout the period of making the book, is to show the child that you are interested in him or her and that there is no limit to what you can be told. You can make it clear that you would like to know lots more about him or her and so will be visiting regularly and getting to know them.

Remember that you are talking to a person who happens to be a child and a client. This means that he or she is as about as interested in telling you about how they are getting on at school as you would be in telling a stranger about how you are getting on at work. Every other adult will have asked them how they get on at school, and they know it is just a conversational ploy used by strangers. When you have got to know the child and he or she knows you are genuinely interested, they may tell you honestly how they feel about school.

You need not say anything of great meaning at first, but simply convey that you will be coming to talk to the child about him or herself and to complete a life

story book. Each child will work at a different pace, just like adults, and you should allow the work to happen naturally; any child will let you know when they want to be friends with you.

2. Should you feel the need to approach the idea of making a life story book cautiously or slowly, you could start with a questionnaire book, which we describe later.

3. When the work on the life story book is undertaken by someone not living with the child, it should always take place at set times which you *faithfully keep*. Don't just say, 'I'll see you in a week or two'. Make a date and keep to it. If you cannot keep an appointment, ring up and speak to the child personally, say why you cannot come and say when you are going to come next. You will probably be the first person in the child's life to do this and it will bring forward the day when he or she learns to trust you.

4. If you are living with the child, you should be able to talk together at any time that is mutually convenient. In addition there should be regular times set aside so that the child does not have to be responsible for continuing the book alone. You must not just allow the topic to drift and find that weeks go by without the book moving on.

Initial research

You need to inform yourself about the child's 'official' background before you start to work together. If you are a social worker, you will have access to the child's file. If you are an adoptive or foster parent and it has been decided that you will be helping your child to make a life story book, then your child's social worker should provide the information. Don't be afraid to badger until you have all the information you need. If you meet difficulties, exercise your right to call a review to 'iron out' any problems.

Read the information about the child carefully and thoroughly. Collate the information in chronological order, noting the reasons given for decisions, the reasons for moves and so on. Make a note of any gaps in the records so that you can obtain information about these periods. From this research you will be able to construct a 'life graph' for the child. We show an example on page 25, when we discuss life graphs in detail.

Using the information you have gathered, write *immediately* to significant people in the child's life. (They may take time to respond and you want to have this information available when you need it.) Explain about the planned life story book and ask for infor-

mation and the loan of photographs and other documents. It is important to emphasise that photographs can be copied and returned to the sender, or that they can send copies.

We give below a sample of the kind of letter that you might send in order to get such information.

The material you ask for may well be very slow to arrive or may never arrive and you will have to depend upon other aids.

Following up the background

Whenever possible, the child's social worker should visit significant people in the child's life to gather further information to help to form as complete a picture as possible. These people may include the natural parents and wider family, children's home staff and former foster parents. Again you will need to write first to let them know the purpose of your visit.

Birth parents and their extended family
Do not be afraid to approach birth parents, even if it is a long time since they saw their child. Those involved with a child are usually anxious about this. They may say, 'She has forgotten her mother . . . Why stir up the

12

Mrs M Croft
7 New Town Estate
Westfield

Dear Mrs Croft

I have recently started visiting David to help him prepare a book about his life before he came to live at Eastfield Children's Home. Already I have obtained several photographs for him to include but I have no photographs of when he was very young, nor any of you.

Photographs, I realise, are very precious but nowadays they can be easily copied. If you have any photographs I would be grateful if you would loan them to me and I would return them as soon as I had obtained copies.

I look forward to hearing from you and perhaps coming to tell you more about David's book.

Yours sincerely

PUPIL CROFT David

David's main pr
confidence; he is
discussions. This also lack
which is often espec
to literature enough
muster up feels ab
thinks or make a con
must improve

ATTENDANCE ACTUAL 48 POSSIBLE
HOMEWORK REGULARITY Good QUAL

past? . . . It will only push her mother into making trouble . . .' Such worries are genuine. Obviously a birth parent should not be approached if this might cause harm to the child, but be sure of your own motivation if you decide not to ask for the birth parents' help. Is it to protect the child or to protect yourself?

When we first started to approach natural parents we, too, were worried about the damage we might cause. Perhaps we have been lucky, but we have never ceased to be amazed by birth parents' willingness to cooperate.

Usually it is only the birth family which can provide the information to make a family tree, one of the best ways of showing a child where he or she 'came from', which we discuss later.

Often, when a child is illegitimate, the birth mother will provide information about the birth father. Perhaps it will be the first time she has been asked about him in a way that seems relevant to her. She might reveal such insights for the child as 'He had blue eyes', 'He was six foot tall', 'He loved the country-side', 'He was good with animals'. It is unlikely that, in her contact with officials, she will ever have been asked for this kind of information.

She might, too, provide an account of her own child-hood. This can often help her child to understand and come to terms with being unable to live with her. Sometimes the child will learn that one parent has either been in care too or had an unhappy childhood.

Children's home staff
Many children will have lived in several children's homes. Staff, especially cooks, cleaners and garden-ers, who have worked in a home a long time, will have photographs which you can borrow. These may be of the child in a group, or of the staff or of the home itself.

Foster parents
If a child has lived in a foster family, they will often have photographs of the child and the family. They are also a source of information which can be in-cluded in the life story book.

Be prepared to exercise imagination and flair in obtaining photographs, treasures, school work, old toys — anything that helps children to understand that they have a past and gives them a sense of identity and belonging.

13

There is no set procedure for how you work on a life story book. The approach we take may not be suitable for you, and you will discover your own approach.

Meeting the child

Unless you are the child's foster or adoptive parent, the child becomes your client as a social worker. Each session should focus on the task of getting to know the child in order to make progress with the life story book. This means – and we repeat this because it is so important – that you become a regular, reliable and predictable person in the child's life. Make appointments and keep them.

David whose life story book is used to illustrate this booklet, obviously thought that adults were untrustworthy and unreliable. He said at our eighth meeting, 'You always come on the day you say you will, don't you?'

How long should a session last?

The length of a session will depend on a number of factors: whether the child lives with you, the child's span of concentration, the time you have available. Ideally, you should set a specific time for each session. We find that an hour is perhaps the maximum time we can hold our own concentration, and, for this reason, we usually structure the session to last roughly that long.

If the child lives with you, perhaps the weekend is the best time for these sessions because you both may be more relaxed and free from week-day pressures.

How often will you meet?

Kay Donley in her 'Ten Commandments' states that you should become a regular and consistent person in your child's life. What is meant by 'regular'? We feel that in the early stages, say the first eight to ten weeks of working with a child, you should aim for weekly sessions. However, you may find that once a fortnight, though less satisfactory, is more realistic. Try to avoid raising your child's expectations by frequent contact in the first three or four weeks and then becoming erratic in your later contact.

Surprisingly, if you are either a residential social worker or a foster or adoptive parent and your child

lives with you, it can be difficult to arrange regular sessions. It is often a problem to find a mutually convenient time within the domestic and social rhythms of the household. A person outside the household can interrupt these rhythms more easily. A foster parent's free time can clash with a child's time, for example, when he or she wants either to watch television or play out with friends.

The most important aim is that the life story book is started and the sessions on it are consistent. It may seem a large commitment and this could deter you. Vera Fahlberg states that 'tomorrow is made harder by lack of preparation today'; in other words, this is time well spent and may eventually save you time by helping to ensure that your child's placement does not break down.

What materials do you need?

Apart from the photographs and other documents, all you need is a looseleaf folder and paper and it is useful to have pens, coloured pencils and glue handy for drawing, writing and putting pictures into the folder. A looseleaf folder allows you to make corrections and to add new material as it comes to light.

Children in care often experience educational difficulties and it's important that they are not made to struggle with writing in their life story books. You can help them with spelling, if requested, but avoid correcting any mistakes. Some children enjoy dictating, for you to write or type; or you could write in pencil for the child to go over in ink. Always remember that this is the child's own private book, not a show piece. Be prepared for it to be somewhat untidy and messy and allow the child to include anything he or she wants.

Who else should be involved?

You need to work away from distractions and interruptions. However, it is important to have another adult involved in the work, although not part of the session. For example, if you are a foster parent, the child's social worker will have to provide most of the factual information and seek out photographs. As the work progresses, the child might wish to show and talk about the life story to this significant adult, who has helped in this way. Doing so may help you to ascertain how the child is absorbing and understanding the past.

Who keeps the life story book?

Without question the book belongs to the child. Should he or she, therefore, be allowed to keep it? Of course, but the timing is important. Some would argue that as the book belongs to them, the child should *always* keep it. This is the ideal and should certainly be what happens towards the end of the time you are working together. However, at certain stages some children destroy their life story book if it is in their possession. The child may be overwhelmed by a sense of anger and frustration about what has happened and may direct this at the book. If this happens, valuable photographs and documents may be lost forever. (We now take photocopies of documents which cannot be replaced.) In the early stages, therefore, we recommend that you are prudent and make sure that the book is kept in a safe place. At all times the child should have reasonable access to it, but this needs to be supervised.

You may decide to provide a photo album separately too, and this alleviates the problem of how to keep the book safely and yet share it with your child.

Usually we find that the best time to give the book into a child's own keeping is when the child has joined the new family and is showing signs of being secure with them. Then the life story book may well become a proud possession which the child wants to show to others. A social worker in Northern Ireland comments in *Life Books for Children in Care*, 'Through their life books, our children have come to own their own story little by little, mainly because they have gone through them so often with other people and each time it becomes clearer to them. Besides, in re-telling it, they think of new questions to ask and gain new realisations each time.'[*]

Who can read the life story book?

The answer is no one – without the child's permission. This, of course, is another element of confidentiality. Nonetheless, encouraging the child to share his or her book should be a feature of your work. For example, foster parents might suggest that their child talk about the book with their social worker. If the child agrees, it can provide an opportunity to talk about events in their life. An additional bonus can be that the person

15

[*]Northern Ireland Foster Care Association, 362 Antrim Road, Belfast BT15 5AE (1984).

who is helping the child make the book can gauge the level of understanding from the way their child talks about the past. But you must be sure that the child really wants to share the book and is not just agreeing to please you.

It is implicit from the beginning of making a life story book, where the plan is to place a child in a new family, that the new family will be shown the book. This is made easier because we always include the child's anxieties and aspirations for the future in the book. For example, the child's desire to own a bicycle or to remain in contact with someone from the past. One girl, worried about how she might be punished by her new parents, wrote in her book, 'It is alright to be smacked, but not to be hit with a belt'. Through the life story book, children can have a safe way of making known their expectations to their new family.

We have found that, as they move towards placement, many children allow their prospective family to look at their book. From the other side, we encourage the prospective families to make their own life story book for the child to see. Children appreciate this gesture and it can be a very good 'ice breaker'.

How will the work affect you?

As we have said before, you should never betray the child's confidences and should not avoid talking about the things the child wants to talk about because they make *you* feel uncomfortable.

Most of us have also experienced feelings of loss and separation. Working with children who are unravelling their own sufferings may release some of these feelings within yourself. It is important that you have the help of someone you can talk to about what is happening to you. If you are a foster parent, your local foster parent group may be able to help. Some of these groups hold regular meetings for foster parents who are helping their children to make life story books. Other people may turn to the child's social worker for support, and social workers to their colleagues.

What problems will you face?

In taking on the work of making a life story book, you can expect some regression from the child as a matter of course. By 'regression' we mean a return to behaviour which might have been left behind, or taking on behaviour patterns which belong to a much younger age group. A common experience, for example, is that the child's behaviour will go back to that appropriate for the age at which they were admitted to care.

Everyone has their own way of dealing with these problems. However, regressive behaviour will not persist and we have never taken it as a sign that we should discontinue the life story book. If children find that the life story book is too threatening, they simply will not do the book and will make it quite clear to you, not simply regress for a period. (We discuss regression further in the next section.)

Be honest, but not brutal

Every child is hurt by being removed from their family. Use this knowledge in talking to the child. Many of the other adults in a child's life may tell you that he or she is completely untouched by it and never wants to talk about it. You must know better, and work to allow the child to express this hurt and anger at some stage. They will want to do this, but may never have found anyone who has been trustworthy enough to tell. You may be the first person who has gained their trust in being consistent in wanting to know all about them.

Don't impose your version of events on the child, as many adults will have done. You want to find out what the child thinks about what has happened. If you disagree with what you think is fantasy, say so, but be no more authoritative than you would be in disagreeing with another adult.

Be honest, but not brutal. If you cover up or prevaricate, the child will know it and will not trust you as much. If you side with children in running down their parents or others, you will find later that they will not be honest with you about talking about their past or their feelings about others. Try to find some positive thing about people they complain about, but don't cover up the negatives. Try to be even-handed and objective about why people do things and children will trust you more than if you join in a tirade against their family and friends. Remember that their natural family is part of them: criticising the family will eventually feel like criticism of *them*.

Finally, remember that every child is an individual with a very interesting story to tell if you can help them to do it. Let them know that you are interested and can be trusted and eventually they will want to talk to you all about themselves.

16

5 Some questions answered

We have made it clear throughout that making a life story book with a child in care can be fraught with difficulties. If you are aware of some of these difficulties, you will be more able to face them together should you meet them. We pose here some of the questions which may arise.

My child was battered as a toddler. How do I explain that?

We are frequently asked how you tell a child potentially unpleasant things about his or her parents. It is easier to answer this by giving some examples of what you should *not* say:

Your birth mother loved you very much, but she had not enough money to look after you because she had no job.

What happens then if either wage earner in a new family is made redundant? And how do you explain birth parents who are now working?

Your first mummy became ill, that is why you came to live with us, but she still loves you.

What happens then when either you become ill or the birth mother gets better?

What may appear to be an act of kindness to protect a child is often an excuse to avoid a painful issue by the adult involved. The motto 'Knowledge expels fear' comes from a parachute school, but it is transferable to assisting a child to understand the past.

A child growing up in the love and security of a family would normally have knowledge and understanding of most of the events in that family's life. Not to have such information and knowledge can lead to confusion, unhappiness, misery.

There is often a very real sense of void. Some children have talked about a 'physical emptiness'; others about a 'knot' inside them. Knowledge can fill a void; understanding dispel what is often an irrational fear and untie the knot. We know from adults who have been adopted as babies that to stumble on the knowledge of their adoption in later life can have a devastating effect. The very foundation that their lives are built on suddenly turns to sand. It is better gradually to face reality as a child and come to terms with it.

When your problem is how to explain why your child was battered, there is no easy solution, but lying about it won't help.

With the younger child, you need give little detail in the early stages, but gradually provide more detail in response to questions as the child gets older. Children often ask what they want to know, not what you want to tell them. Listen to the questions carefully and answer what the child has *asked*. Kay Donley says that the information given should be 'age appropriate'.

David had been received into care because it was considered that his mother had neglected him. Yet she was neither bad nor wicked, more a victim of circumstances. Before we talked to David about this, we had obtained a family tree from her. From this, her own unhappy childhood came to light. She talked about struggling alone with David in a bedsitter, a 17 year old with no help and little money.

17

Me with my mum. I was three months old.

Once we understood this, we talked together as a team about how we should explain events to David. This is what we told him:

Mary, your birth mum, had an unhappy childhood; she spent some time in a children's home herself. When you were born, she lived with her mother for a while, but decided to try to live in a bedsitter with you alone. She was all on her own without any help. Sometimes, because she was lonely, she went out and left you on your own. At other times, when you cried as all young children do, she smacked you too hard and bruised you. She was not a bad person, but did not know how to look after young children.

It is very difficult to present the fact objectively, especially when the child's birth parents appear to have few redeeming features, but it is important that you should try to give a balanced view in keeping with the child's age and ability to understand events.

If children know they can ask questions about the past freely throughout their childhood, you will have removed a major source of potential difficulty. The past will no longer be a mystery, not to be discussed. You will have brought it down to being normal, everyday and ordinary.

Children who have suffered many separations will blame themselves and believe that they are bad. If their parents were 'bad', it must mean they have inherited this 'badness'. They may even believe they were the cause of their parents' 'badness'. If you can help your child to understand the events and circumstances of the past, that will go a long way to healing the deep wounds of the hurt that has been suffered.

What if my child begins to lose interest in the life story book?

From time to time during the course of making a life story book, the child's interest will wane. Our descriptive illustrations in this book are only 'edited highlights'. We have spent many sessions when little progress seems to have been made. This need not worry you.

There will be periods when nothing much is said or done during your sessions. If you are arriving at the same time each week or fortnight, you will have little control over what mood the child is in. If you force the pace, the life story book will become unpleasant for the child and that is not what you want. Of course, if the child is living with you, it is possible to choose moments to work together when the child wishes to respond, but even so there may be periods when the work is very slow.

All the time that you are helping a child, you need someone with whom to discuss events, and this is especially necessary when you are in the doldrums. There are some play techniques you can introduce (which we discuss in Section 9), but we only start to use them after discussion with the colleagues and friends who are providing us with support.

What if my child regresses?

We have said already that, during the making of a life story book, the child's behaviour may move backward until it is more appropriate to that of a younger child. You should be prepared for this. Regression can take a whole range and variety of forms. Bed wetting and soiling, temper tantrums, becoming quiet and withdrawn are just a few.

One 12 year old boy insisted on being carried to bed each evening. Gradually this changed to being 'chased' to bed and, eventually, he went to bed 'normally'. During this period he also presented problems at school: shouting out in class, scribbling in his exercise books whenever his work was criticised. His foster parents regarded his developmental age at this period as being that of a six year old.[*]

This regression is to be expected. It is a normal reaction. The movement backwards is usually short lived and from it comes a healthy growth. It is important to know that your child may regress and that you may need help through difficult patches from other foster parents or your social worker, if you are the foster parent, or from colleagues if you are the worker involved.

With my first mum. She used to cuddle me.

---

[*]See Vera Fahlberg's *Child Development* (BAAF 1982) for a detailed explanation of development stages.

18

6 Helping the child to talk about feelings

You will find as you work that the child will dictate the pace. Some of what is revealed will be distressing to both of you. If you are at a loss as to how to respond to this distress in words, physical affection or a sympathetic smile help children to feel that you are on their side and are not put off by them or their past.

We have found that it is necessary from the beginning to establish that you are aware that the child has good/bad, happy/sad, positive/negative feelings, and it is vital to establish that the child is aware that it is safe to talk about the bad as well as the good.

There are approaches which we have found useful in displaying that you accept these opposite emotions. Try to make it interesting and even enjoyable for children to express themselves by getting them to make things and draw pictures. We describe here how we have worked through pictures to help children to talk about feelings in a way that is safe for them. Violet Oaklander in her book *Windows to our Children* (Real People Press, 1978) suggests and explains many further useful ideas that can help children to express these emotions.

Using questionnaires

A 'questionnaire' is a set of questions or unfinished sentences, like those shown in this illustration, which the child can answer, react to and discuss. A questionnaire can be useful in several ways in the early stages of working with a child on a life story.

I like my......
I hate it when..
I am afraid to..
My face has a
big smile when..
I hate to eat...
I hope that.....

Because of the structured nature of questionnaires, less demand is made on the child to be forthcoming and inventive. It is therefore particularly useful for children not used to writing down their thoughts or whose literacy is limited. For these children and for those who find it difficult to express themselves, for whatever reason, the questionnaire method can be used as a prelude to the life story book itself and put into the front of the book proper.

The structure of questionnaires is a matter of your choice. You can buy questionnaire booklets with attractive covers.* Some of these are simply lists of questions progressing in sensitivity from fairly neutral questions, such as:

What is your favourite colour?
Which colour don't you like?

to progressively more sensitive questions, such as:

Who is your favourite person?
Who is your least favourite person?
Which person do you dislike most?

These questions lead children into making statements about themselves. They get them used to expressing both negative and positive statements about themselves and also convey the message that you are interested in them.

Some questionnaire books are structured differently and allow more creativity. They may contain, for example, a blank page with the heading, 'This is a picture of my favourite person' or 'This is how I see myself', allowing children to draw pictures expressing aspects of themselves or their hopes and fears.

You can use the questionnaire idea imaginatively by constructing one yourself, encouraging the child to illustrate the cover with photos, drawings, elaborate writing or stick-on paper shapes. If you construct a questionnaire booklet yourself you can make it lead into areas which will be helpful for the child. One obvious idea is to omit negative statements altogether if you are working with a child who seems to have a wholly negative image of him or herself. Thus the questionnaire booklet when completed will contain only positive statements about the child.

19

Got to be me! Merrill Harmin, Argus Communications, Niles, Illinois, USA, 1976.
This is me! Merrill Harmin, Argus Communications, 1977.
The Anti-Colouring Book Susan Striker and Edward Kimmel, Scholastic Publications, London, 1978.

Questionnaires can be structured to help a child to think about the future, with questions such as:

When I grow up I will live in . . .
When I leave this children's home I will feel . . .
When I go to a new family, it will help me to . . .

The possibilities are endless. Don't forget, however, that questionnaires are only an adjunct or preliminary to life story books, which allow freer discussion and a wider ranging expression of views than question-naires do by themselves.

In using questionnaires we avoid trying to interpret the answers back to the child. The answers to some questions may be very significant, or appear so, but to go into them in depth at an early stage would unsettle some children and might warn them off opening up and revealing their inner and private world. In other words, don't push too early.

Using pictures to enable a child to talk about feelings

Invite the child to draw a picture of him- or herself and the things they like best which make them happy. Encourage them to write a caption to the picture about these happy/enjoyable events or to dictate such a caption for you to write. Try not to lead them or to search for any hidden meaning. Keep the activity simple and reproduce the child's own words.

I like to write

I don't like going to bed.

Once this is completed to the child's satisfaction, suggest that he or she draws a picture of something they hate to do or which makes them angry. Usually children deny that anything makes them angry or sad, or that there is anything they hate. Often it has not been safe to show these feelings, so to deny them is normal. Don't push this issue.

Some children will respond with 'safe' dislikes. A six-year-old girl wrote 'I do not like those yellow things at school'. We later found that she meant the sweet corn occasionally served with school dinners. You might encourage a listing of 'safe' things that are hated, like cabbage, plums or 'those yellow things'.

All that you are doing at this stage is to show that you are aware that the child has both positive and negative feelings and that you accept both unconditionally. Sometimes there is resistance to drawing pictures, but we have successfully 'broken the ice' with the question-naire method and the happy/sad face.

The happy/sad face

This face is made from two paper plates. One of them is cut in half and hinged to the back of the other so that it can be alternated (see opposite page).

The child – or you – can draw a happy face on the full plate. Then the half plate is turned over and either a sad or an angry face drawn on it. With this it is then possible to ask, 'Who are you today? Are you Miss Happy or Miss Sad?'

We have taken this further by asking the child to describe how 'the face' might be feeling inside. If the child can do this we write their comments on the 'feelings' cards (see below). You should avoid rushing this stage, especially if it is early in your work with the child.

'Feelings' cards

In order to express emotions, children need a reper-toire of words which they feel comfortable using. Providing words to describe these feelings can be difficult, for the child will resist acknowledging that such emotions exist. Vera Fahlberg in her film *Adoptive children, adaptive feelings* demonstrates a tech-nique she has developed; the use of 'feelings' cards. These are a set of cards each of which has a single word which identifies a specific emotional response.

22

We have taken this idea and used it with an individual child and with groups of children by making the initial introduction of these words into a game. The child (or children) is encouraged to call out words that describe an emotion and these words are written onto blank cards. The words may be, for example, good, bad, happy, sad, miserable, cheerful, kind, cruel. Once sufficient words have been gathered, the 'game' continues with the child drawing a face to match each 'feelings' word (see above).

This is a helpful exercise because it familiarises children with emotive words and gradually sensitises them to using these words to describe their feelings about situations and events. Introduced in this way, the potential threat and danger children may experience when attempts are made to attribute such feelings to them are avoided.

For example, when you are later talking about an incident in the child's past, the cards can be laid out and the child can be encouraged to pick out a card that describes how they felt at the time. This method could be used when a child is describing how they felt at leaving a particular foster home and perhaps how they feel about it now. In this way past trauma can often be gradually resolved.

Throughout your work together, you can refer back to the cards from time to time and ask the child to add more words.

What will the child get from these sessions?

Don't be worried by what appears to be a lack of emotional response at this stage. Drawing the good/bad pictures has an impact that will not become apparent until much later in the life story book work.

Avoid making any interpretation of the drawings, and accept a child's statement that they cannot think of anything that makes them angry. If they do disclose a small portion of their inner world, let it pass at this meeting, but make a note of it to be used as a reference point later. For example, when a child is starting to discuss feelings of loss, you might say, 'Do you remember when you drew a happy picture and could think of nothing that made you angry? I think that you feel angry because Anne lives with Mary, your 'born to' mother, and you do not.'

7 Some elements of a life story book

There are various elements which may be included in a life story book. We list them here and then go on to discuss them in detail.

Where I came from   My life graph
My birth certificate   Visiting the past
My family tree   Photographs about me
My own map

We illustrate how these elements work with examples from the life story book of 'David' who made a life story book with one of us some years ago when he was eight.

Where I came from

Once we assumed that most children know where babies come from. Now we know that this is not the case, and you will have to discover how much your child actually knows before you talk about this. Mother and baby books from either your local health centre or library should provide all the visual aids necessary to cover the period from conception to the first birthday.

David was, fortunately, aware that a baby grows in its mother's tummy and, from there, it was a simple step to establish that he started to grow in Mary's (his born to mother) tummy when John planted his seed.

A boby growing in its mothers tummy. I grew in Mory's tummy.

At this early stage, because photographs from relatives, foster parents and others may be slow to arrive, you will have to improvise, returning to fill in details later.

The hospital where the child was born will provide the time of birth and the weight at birth. You can give this information direct to the older child, but a younger child needs to be helped to understand it. The child can draw a clock face showing the time of birth and can stick in the book the equivalent of the birth weight in, say, pictures of bags of sugar.

23

When I was born I weighted 3.4 Kilograms which is like 3 bags of sugar

The child can draw or collect pictures of very young children and give them captions. For example:

This is my drawing of a baby at six months. I might have looked like this.

I had my first birthday party at Oak Street where I lived with John and Mary, my born to dad and mum.

My birth certificate

When we first started to work with children by helping them to make life story books, we provided a photo-copy of their birth certificate to complete the part about their birth. We thought it would only be of passing interest to them. We were not prepared for the potent effect it had. Now we find it usually occupies a whole session. It is of immense interest to the children and can provoke numerous questions. Even small children who cannot read seem to grasp its significance to them, that it is documentary evidence that they were born and have an identity which can never be taken away from them.

At the same time the birth certificate can have a temporarily unsettling effect on adoptive and foster parents. For them, it is also documentary evidence that they are not the 'born to' parents of their child. If you are in this position, remember that there is more to being a parent than giving birth and it is only if you are able to accept the facts of your child's birth that the child will feel accepted by you as his or her new parents.

My family tree

As we have said, the birth family is the best source of information for making a family tree. We consider that its making, showing the child his or her place on it, is very important.

The knowledge of the extended family can be painful to children because it emphasises that they are severed from their birth family and forebears. Nonetheless it can also do a great deal to help children understand some of the events that led to the loss of their family.

By working on his family tree Jimmy, a nine-year-old, could start to understand why he was received into care as a two year old, bruised and neglected. He understood that his mother was sixteen years old when he was born, and that she too had been in care. Jimmy was living in a large children's home in which there were several sixteen year old girls. He began to grasp that his mother was not bad or cruel, just very young and ill-prepared to be a mother to him.

Remember that family patterns are now diverse and it may help children to accept their own situations to know that there are such variations. One marriage in three ends in divorce and one child in five lives in a single parent family. The life story book should not, therefore, attempt to portray a model of family life that is alien to the child and removed from the varying pattern that exists in society.

David's mother, as you can see from his family tree (below), entered into three relationships before she established a stable life for herself. Frequently children come from such changing households with further developments occurring after they have left. These complicated relationships can be an additional source of stress for a child because the changes are difficult to understand.

If the plans are to resettle children back in their birth families, it is important to ensure they have a knowledge and understanding of the changes that have gone on since they left. If the child is not returning to the birth family and the changes in the family are one of the reasons for this, the child needs to understand why. For instance, David was angry because his half-sister Lisa lived with his mother and he did not. There had been an unsuccessful attempt to settle him back with his mother, but the changes in his family meant that they could not assimilate an older child.

24

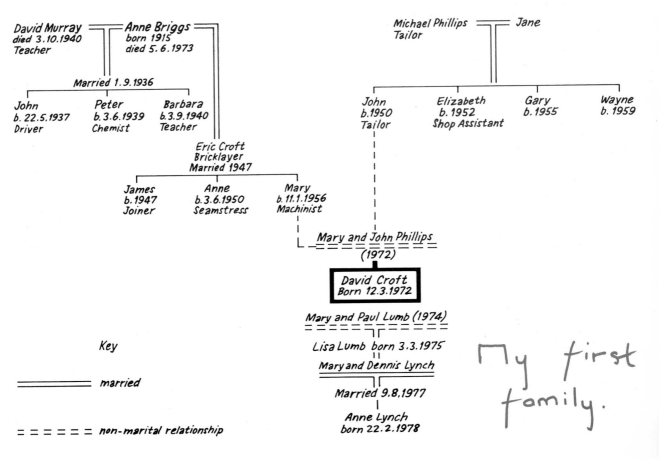

My own map

This is a device we use to provide the child with a sense of movement through time. We map out with the child the moves of the birth family and the child's own moves since leaving them. Often we start with the geographical area where the birth mother was born and lived. This map may help a child to understand part of his or her own predicament – if, for example, the birth mother had an unstable childhood with many moves too. (See example below.)

When working together on a 'map', it is important to remember that a child in care's concept of time will be different to your own. We have found that a child can conceptualise the length of the last school holiday and you can build on this. However, if you say, 'You lived for two years with your mother in this town,' it is likely to mean very little.

My life graph

The father of one of our new families developed this life graph. It is a simple diagram that helps the child, the worker and the new parents to understand the movements in the child's life. When we started using the life graph, we found resistance from children to working in what we saw as logical order, from birth to the present day. To the children this was not logical. For them it was simpler to work back through time, starting from the present.

Again, you can write the entries in pencil for the child to ink over. David chose to leave the painful recent past till last (see below). Using different pens for colour-coding the different types of care (with natural parents, with foster parents, etc), can clarify the graph.

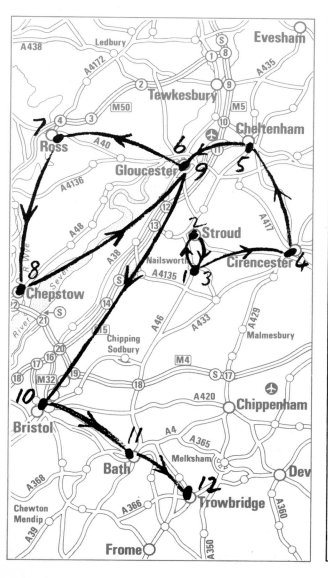

12TH MARCH – BORN IN MATERNITY HOSPITAL 6 P.M. I LIVED WITH MARY, MY BORN TO MOTHER, AND GRANDMOTHER CROFT. WE LIVED AT 117 OAK STREET	1972
MY FIRST BIRTHDAY PARTY 5TH JUNE. GRANDMOTHER CROFT DIED	1973
3RD NOVEMBER. HIGH MEADOW NURSERY MY SECOND BIRTHDAY 5TH MAY. WITH MARY AT 117 OAK STREET	1974
28TH DECEMBER. LEAKE STREET CHILDREN'S HOME 3RD MARCH. LISA LUMB BORN MY THIRD BIRTHDAY 3RD JUNE. WITH MARY AND PAUL LUMB — EASTWOOD ROAD 20TH NOVEMBER. THE CHILDREN'S HOSPITAL 5TH JANUARY. THE HOLLIES CHILDREN'S HOME MY FOURTH BIRTHDAY	1975
24TH DECEMBER. PETER AND JOAN BATT. FOSTER PARENTS MY FIFTH BIRTHDAY	1976
9TH AUGUST. MARY MARRIES DENNIS LYNCH 22ND FEBRUARY. ANNE LYNCH BORN MY SIXTH BIRTHDAY	1977
	1978
29TH MAY. MARY AND DENNIS LYNCH. DUNCAN TERRACE	1979
5TH JANUARY. MOVED WITH FAMILY TO NEWTOWN GATE 2ND FEBRUARY. THE HAVEN CHILDREN'S HOME 30TH MAY. EASTFIELD ASSESSMENT CENTRE	1980
12TH NOVEMBER. WITH CHRIS AND EDDIE	1981

This is me on 30th September 1981 outside the maternity hospital where I was born.

On the way through the life graph there will be painful events which children will want to avoid talking about in the early stages, but will eventually come to them when they are feeling stronger and more secure. We always prepare life graphs in pencil and introduce them when we are talking about the child's birth, suggesting that they ink over that first entry. In the next session, the child inks in the last entry, which is the present day. From there, we ask them to ink in any section they wish and we talk about this section together.

At first most children will only be prepared to consider the less troubled periods of their lives, so do not expect any startling revelations. As the child inks over the 'safe' periods, the uncompleted parts will indicate the periods about which they are unhappy and troubled.

Younger children, who cannot yet read or write, can be encouraged to colour each segment of time. We find that this helps them to understand time and events. Birthdays are useful for marking the passage of time, especially when they are something about which the child may have happy memories.

The life graph can be varied to suit the needs of the child. We know of foster parents who have prepared a life graph of the birth parents too, so that the child can understand what was happening to them as well.

Visiting the past

Many children deny that events in their past have happened. The uncompleted sections on the life graph may indicate to you where their problems lie. If you are satisfied that children like this are familiar with many aspects of the life graph, we believe that taking them on a trip to visit all the places they have lived in can help to overcome this difficulty.

Such visits will entail careful preparation, not only of the child, but also of the people from the past, and must be carefully timed. It should never be a substitute for the actual life story book work but an accompaniment to it. If we can accomplish the visits in one day we do so. The preparations will take longer and the work involved invariably means that the journey will have to be arranged by the child's social worker, who may need to make preliminary visits in order to prepare and explain the purpose of the contact.

Whenever possible on these trips, work backward from the present using the child's life graph and personal map. This physical and geographical tracing of the child's life assists and enables them to place their life in context. It is invaluable in assisting you too, and it is inevitably a moving experience for all concerned.

An unexpected bonus for us has been the warmth, affection and welcome received at each stopping place. Often children may have left these places abruptly, believing they have harmed and damaged people. To discover that they have not can be a relief and, therefore, an additional dividend.

At a later stage when 'bridging' children into the future (see page 30) and using the candle technique (see page 32), we are able to refer back to this journey and to the positive benefits to the children of having people in their past who loved them.

Me with Tony outside number 117 Ook Street where I lived with Mary. It's empty now.

Me outside my primary school. I went there when I lived with the Botts.

We also use these trips to simulate photographs of earlier events, which are captioned in the life story book, as David's shows here.

How these visits help children to begin to acknowledge their past and to face up to painful events in their lives showed clearly with David. He had denied any knowledge of the time he spent at High Meadow Nursery even when he was taken there. For him to admit he had lived there was to acknowledge that his mother had been unable to care for him adequately.

The cook and matron remembered him with affection and told tales of his early childhood — normally the function of parents. Afterwards, David walked upstairs and into a bedroom, and said: 'That was my bed and I used to watch the trains from that window.'

Photographs about me

Photographs are an invaluable and essential part of any life story book. They are not only a record of past events but also a means by which a child may be able to talk about the past and express feelings about it. However, you must avoid the trap of turning a life story book into a photograph album with captions. The photographs are there to provide you with a focus for working together. We suggest that you may, alongside the life story book, help the child to make a separate album of photographs.

Although children will be interested in the photographs, they may be reluctant to use the sensitive ones in the life story book. David asked to keep the photograph of his natural mother and was allowed to do so, but we retained copies too as we were uncertain

about whether or not he would destroy the others because they raised such painful memories.

A photograph can be stuck on to a blank sheet of paper and used alongside the life graph and family tree. The child can write captions to the photo which link their knowledge of all three components.

David dictated under a photograph taken at Christmas 1979:

I spent Christmas with my mum, Lisa, Anne and Dennis at New Town Estate. Lisa and Anne got bikes and I got a toy car. It's not fair, Lisa and Anne live with my mum and I don't. Dennis is okay, he used to give me rides on his motorbike. My mum used to shout and hit me with a belt. It's not fair Mr Hughes and the staff at Eastfield keep me from going home to my mum. I hate them. When I was with my mum I jumped on the settee and made a hole in it.

David dictated at another session:

August 1974. This is me on a donkey at Filey. I went with my mum, Lisa, Uncle James and Paul Lumb for the day. My mum was not a bad person. She was not good looking after little ones.

The photographs of his mother had a deep emotional impact, but he eventually placed them in his life story book and dictated, 'Mary wants me to be adopted but I want Mary to adopt me.'

At the following session he dictated:

This is my first Mum Mary and my dog. She gave the dog away. It made me sad because she gave the dog away. It makes me sad because I cannot live without her.

David's captions show how photographs help a child to talk about and express feelings. Certain photo-

28

Me as a baby
with my born to
Dad. I have brown
eyes like him.

Lisa eating
melon at Filey.

graphs will be more significant because of the importance the child attaches to them. For example, we
spent two sessions on the three photographs of
David's mother, whereas seven pictures of his foster
parents were dealt with in half a session. The reason
for this was that the photographs of David's mother
provided a means of discussing his relationship with
her, the hurt he felt at not living with her and a
movement towards realising that to return to her was
not possible. It was a start at helping him to understand that his mother cared *about* him even though her
circumstances meant she could not care *for* him.

David was obviously pleased with all his photographs
and wanted to show them and share them with his
friends. This raised another problem. His life story
book contained information which was personal and
confidential, not for general consumption. How
could he share the photographs but not the information? We asked ourselves how our own children did
this: the answer was by using the family album. David
was provided with a separate album to share.

Me with Steven
and Graham Bott.
I lived with
them from 1976
to 1978.

Thomas, Mary and Nellie: their life story book

This case study shows how the life story book with its visits and photographs worked for one child.

Thomas was 13 years old when he was placed with Mary, a single woman in her late 40's and her widowed mother. It was his ninth placement and he came direct to them from his third foster home breakdown.

Thomas's parents separated before he was born. His mother, who already had one child, was estranged from her extended family and without help or support. She left Thomas in the hospital where he was born, believing he would be adopted. Thomas was placed with elderly foster parents, and stayed with them for eight years until he was removed because he was refusing to go to school.

What follows is an account of how we untangled and came to understand Thomas's past through a life story book.

Thomas wrote in his life story book, 'My first foster mother, who I thought was my real mum, used to spoil me. She let me do anything. We used to tie sheets together and play at Tarzan. The social worker took me on holiday because I asked him if he would. He took me to a children's home. I was upset when I found out I was not going back to my foster mother.'

It was very difficult to make Thomas's life story book because we had only photographs from his first foster home and one photograph taken in a children's home when he was ten years old. Very little was known about his birth parents. There was only one thing to do: visit the area around the south coast where he had spent most of his life and experienced three foster homes and five children's homes. This Mary, Thomas and I, as his social worker, did, starting with the maternity hospital where he was born.

Thomas wrote afterwards, 'My mum asked me if I would like to go to my home town to see all my old friends and children's homes which I had stayed in. I am happy at home with my mum, Grandma and the dogs. There are lots of things that have happened that I would rather like to forget, but I did want to show mum and grandma where I used to play, the shops, park and seaside.'

Mary wrote too, 'I was surprised that Thomas could remember so much about the area, he seemed to know where every street and road came out — Thomas had come to life, this was where he had enjoyed himself as a young lad. I

could not help but feel happy for him as we strolled around hand in hand.'

The day was exhausting, enjoyable and rewarding. Move after move, yet Thomas was welcomed back with genuine affection at each place we visited. Mary said afterwards that it laid to rest a lot of ghosts: it helped her to understand and become closer to Thomas but it also made her feel angry at what had happened to her 'son'.

After this the next major step did not seem so big. I traced and visited Jane, his birth mother, who had last seen him as a baby. Taking my camera with me I explained about Thomas's life story book and she willingly allowed me to photograph her. In exchange I gave her recent photographs of Thomas. Jane was now re-married with two children, her oldest child living with her first husband. She also provided detailed information about her own family and I was able to give this to Thomas for his life story book.

The next step was to arrange a meeting between Thomas and Mary with Jane and her second husband and family. This was done and, at the same time, Jane signed her consent for Mary to adopt Thomas. This meeting, which was fraught with potential risks, went smoothly from the moment Thomas produced his life story book to show Jane.

From there, a meeting was arranged with Graham, Thomas's birth father, and Mary and Thomas. Again information was provided for Thomas's family tree: he had been named after Graham's younger brother. Graham too signed the consent to the adoption application.

(It should be stressed that these meetings were only arranged after all the participants clearly understood the purpose. At no time was it to test out whether Thomas could be reunited with his birth parents. It was for Thomas's sake to dispel any secret dreams and fears he might have had about them and to free him emotionally from his past.)

Fifteen months after Thomas went to live with Mary, she adopted him. Two months after this Mary allowed him to spend a week with Jane and her family. (Mary enjoyed not having to ask a social worker for permission.) The following week Mary and 'gran' Nellie collected Thomas and his half-brother and sister and took them to spend a week with Graham, who now lives with his parents and his elder son.

For the first time in his life Thomas is enjoying school, self-assured, confident and secure in the knowledge that Mary loves him. We rarely talk about the past now: there is too much happening in the present and much to look forward to in the future.

8 Bridging: past, present and future

We use the name 'bridging' for the time when we link the past and the present and provide a bridge to the future. We have slowly, from our own experience, come to the conclusion that successfully 'bridging' children is a crucial factor in them remaining in their permanent substitute family.

In working together to make a life story book, you will have gained unique insight and information about the child's past. This will prove invaluable in preparing the new family before the child arrives.

Leaving the present situation to move either to a new family or to return to a birth family is a stressful time for children and they need help and support to cross the 'bridge'. It is a time when past, present and future can be placed in context and 'ghosts' and fantasies laid to rest.

Vera Fahlberg suggests, and we too have found, that a child about to move into a new family is in a state of aroused anxiety, but that it is often possible to deal with earlier unresolved attachment and separation feelings by talking about a child's life experiences through reading the life story book together.

Kay Donley considers that appropriate bridging messages should be incorporated throughout the life story book. She has identified the task, at this stage and in the early stages of placement, as one of disengaging the child from significant parental figures in the past, usually the birth mother, and assisting the child to engage with the 'new' mother. Vera Fahlberg describes the process as one of obtaining 'emotional permission' in order that the child can attach him or herself to the new family. Within the child's experiences there will be a hierarchy of people, starting with the birth mother, who can signal the message of disengagement and start the process of emotional permission to move towards a new family.

At this important stage, it is essential to re-read a child's life story book to make sure that you have not overlooked clues about hidden anxieties and worries. For instance, it became evident that the various statements David had written about his mother indicated a strong attachment to her which was a mixture of reality and fantasy. His life story book contained several questionnaires and within these David had specifically mentioned his mother. For example:

The person I most like — my mother
My face has a big smile when — I see my mother
Things I worry about — my mother
I would not like to live without — my mother

David's birth mother had provided information and photographs of his early life. She had been involved in the plans to place him with an adoptive family and had stated she would consent to his adoption. Through her involvement in helping with material for David's life story book, the concept of disengagement and emotional permission was explained to her. When David had lived with his new family for nine months, a 'farewell' meeting was arranged. At this meeting his mother 'signalled' her approval of David's new parents. David was aware that his mother had consented to his adoption and given her 'permission' for him to attach himself to his new family.

It is not always possible to involve birth parents in this way, either because they cannot be found or because they are unwilling to participate. Kay Donley suggests that you go to the next person in the child's hierarchy. This might be either a previous foster parent or another adult with whom the child has made a significant relationship, such as a member of staff in a children's home. She believes that a child's social worker does not have this significance.

An 'Advent' or 'Moving' Calendar

Once children learn that a decision has been made for them either to return to their birth family or be introduced to a new family, their anxiety level rises. One reason for this, we believe, is that children feel that these plans are outside their control. The process of moving therefore becomes frightening and confusing. We have found that making what we call an 'Advent' or 'moving' calendar can reduce the uncertainty that may surround the move.

An Advent calendar has doors and windows that open to reveal aspects of the Christmas season during the 'countdown' period to Christmas Day. In the same way the doors in a 'moving' calendar open up during the 'countdown' to a placement.

Usually visits home or to a new family are planned over several weeks during the period of introductions. The doors in the 'moving' calendar display a date. When they open they reveal a certain amount of specific information. Here is an example of what such a calendar might reveal.

The candles ritual

The candles ritual is a way, at this stage of 'bridging', of demonstrating to children they they have the capacity to love people. Children enjoy rituals and they can be used to help understand a particular idea. We borrowed the candle technique from Claudia Jewett, who describes it in her book, *Adopting the Older Child* (Harvard Common Press, 1978). We have used it on many occasions because it demonstrates to the child that not only have they the capacity to love, but that it is also safe to love others.

32

You use a row of candles to represent all the people the child has loved in his or her life. In front of this row, you place a candle to symbolise the child. While lighting this candle, you explain that it represents the child's birth, when he or she came into the world with an inborn ability to love people. Next, if it is significant, you light the first candle representing the birth mother and explain that this was the first person the child loved.

You continue the process down the line, lighting a candle for each new situation the child moved into and each new person who was loved. Tell the child that, because they were born with the ability to love people, it is not necessary to put out (extinguish) the love of the previous care-taker before loving another.

This technique illustrates how important it is to keep love alive. Usually we only use it when a new family is imminent, for it reveals that it is safe for the child to light the candles belonging to the new family. Once the child is with the new family, we repeat the ritual with the new parents to emphasise how important it is not to extinguish the love the child has for others from the past, because it illuminates the child in the present.

Perhaps David best summed up the experience when he said, 'The candles I have just lit for Christine and Eddie (his new parents) are burning the brightest and Mary's (his birth mother) candle, lit first, is burning down and will gradually fade away.'

Six months later, David's relationship with his new mother was showing signs of strain. She was able to discuss this with him by reminding him of the candle ritual, commenting that perhaps he felt he had been let down by mother figures in the past and now he was afraid to light a candle for her. David was eventually able to recognise this and accept her assurance that it was safe to light her candle.

The ecomap

Vera Fahlberg in her book *Helping children when they must move* (BAAF 1981) describes what is called an ecomap, originally developed as an initial interviewing tool to open communication between the child and social worker. It shows the child and the various people, places and concerns which form a part of his or her life. Children can discuss these elements and how they relate to them and so gain further understanding of their life as a whole and why they are where they are.

We have successfully taken this idea and adapted it for use not only during the bridging period but also when the child is in the new home. Then it becomes a means of helping the child and the new family to understand in pictorial form what we feel is happening. Vera Fahlberg considers it works best with children in the five to twelve age range, but we have used it as effectively with older children.

A child's responses to the question 'Why am I here?' will help you to perceive his or her understanding of their situation. You can then refer to the life story book to discuss the significant people in the child's life and illustrate their present relationship and the type of contact they have. For example:

My birth mum – writes me letters and speaks to me on the telephone
My social worker – telephones me and visits me

After David had been living with his new family for three months, he began to have behavioural problems at school that were so serious that expulsion was threatened. We used David's ecomap to arrive at an understanding of how his behaviour at school was threatening his future with his new family. On the line from his new home to school he drew arrows attacking it, but shortly after this the extremes of his behaviour subsided and whilst difficulties remained for a time, the threat of expulsion was removed.

The 'three parents'

We always use Vera Fahlberg's 'three parents' as a means of helping children during the bridging period. It has many uses, for example demonstrating to children that it is not possible to take away from them what was endowed at birth by their parents.

We quote here from Vera Fahlberg direct.[*] (Note that she uses the term 'foster care' in the American sense, where it covers both our meaning of foster care *and* adoption.)

We believe that much too often children are not told about what is happening to them when they are moved. Foster care may seem familiar and logical to social workers but makes no sense to children. We have developed a method of explaining foster care to children. The idea is to explain the role of the various parents in their lives and to outline who is responsible for what. We draw three circles like those below and give the child an explanation of the different roles of each kind of parent.

33

Birth parent

Life itself
Sex
Physical looks
Intellectual potential
Predisposition for certain diseases
Basic personality type (such as shy, stubborn, active)

Parenting parent

Love
Provide food, toys, clothes
Give hugs and kisses
Disciplines
Takes care of you when sick

Legal parent

Financial responsibility
Safety and security
Where you live
Where you go to school
Sign for operations
Permission to travel abroad
Sign for marriage under age
Sign for going into services under age

[*]Vera Fahlberg, *Helping children when they must move*, British Agencies for Adoption & Fostering, 1981. She acknowledges the work of Marietta Spencer of the Children's Home Society of Minnesota for this idea.

We say that every birth has parents. There can be no changes in birth parents. Each child has one birth mother and one birth father; no one can ever do anything to change this situation. All children in our society also have legal parents. The legal parent makes the major decisions in a child's life. The parenting parent is the person who is available on a day-to-day basis to meet the child's needs for nurture and discipline.

For many children, one set of parents are simultaneously the birth parents, the legal parents and the parenting parents. However, in foster care and adoption these different kinds of job are split up.

34

The child in care still has a set of birth parents. In the case of voluntary reception into care, the legal parent may still be the birth parent, or the legal parenting role may be shared by the birth parent and the agency. For example, the birth parent's signature might be required for an adolescent to join the Army, while the agency might have the right to select the home in which the child lives and the school the child attends.

When parental rights have been terminated by the court, an agency or the court becomes the legal parent. When the child is fostered, the foster parents are the parenting parents. When there are disputes about who should be the legal parent and who should be the parenting parent, a court makes the decision.

When a child is returned to the birth home, but the agency continues to have legal custody, the diagram can help explain responsibilities. The birth parent then is the parenting parent and the birth parent, but aspects of the legal parent role are retained in the agency or the court.

If parental rights are terminated, the child continues to have the same birth parents; he has the agency or court as a legal parent and has foster parents as the parenting parent. When we explain adoption to such a child, we tell him that termination means no one set of parents will again fill all three parenting roles; however, adoption allows us to combine two aspects of parenting – the legal parent and the parenting parent – in one set of parents. The child learns that social workers or courts will no longer make decisions about him; but rather that the set of parents with whom he lives will also be in charge of making the major decisions in his life.

In all cases this method of explanation accepts the fact that the child has a set of birth parents. The acceptance of birth parents and what they mean in a child's life is critical if we are to help children deal with their feelings about separation from birth parents.

Going back to the life story book as a reference point

Life does not run smoothly, so you can expect even a well prepared child to present problems in the new setting. Most of these will be normal behaviour, but occasionally inappropriate behaviour may have its origins in earlier life experiences – for example, David's fear of loving Chris, his adoptive mother. Vera Fahlberg likens the process to that of a telephone switchboard where the child's past becomes plugged into their present and begins to interfere with and distort it. A life story book may help to identify what has led to this problem and the book can be used, at a time of crisis, as a reference point.

Julie, an eleven year old girl, was having difficulties settling into her new family and her new parents were having difficulty adjusting to her too. It was possible to turn to her life story book where similar incidents had occurred and use it as a reference to the difficulties of living in a family. Julie was struggling with assimilating herself into her new family. She had experienced two foster home breakdowns and she was becoming anxious that her third placement was about to disrupt. It was by helping her express these fears and linking them to painful events in her past that she could begin to understand how her past was interfering with her present. Julie then wrote the following:

I want to stay with Margery and John and for them to be my mum and dad. It is hard to build up a new family. When I fell out with my mum and dad I feel upset. He said if I don't change my attitude I will have to go. I want to change my attitude. When I quarrel with my mum it makes me feel miserable. It makes me worried because I might have to leave home. I would like to stay with mum and dad because it is the right place to be. There is nowhere else to go really. I want to cooperate with other people but it is hard to understand how to do this. I got on with my dad alright and I love them both. I won't go on being miserable and having no friends. I don't understand why I can't make friends because I had friends at Eastfield Lodge.

We were able to show this to her new parents and the tension noticeably reduced. Her new parents were able to understand that Julie's behaviour was not deliberate but was brought about by anxieties from her past that had leaked into her present.

9 Beyond life story books

For some children, making a life story book will not be sufficient to penetrate the barrier they have erected to protect their inner and painful world. We have found this particularly with children who have experienced numerous moves which have severely damaged their ability to form and sustain relationships beyond a superficial level. Such children have been called 'emotionally frozen'. Vera Fahlberg defines this as having an over-investment in the past, into which all energies seem to go, creating an emotional imbalance.

The trauma of separation from the birth parent is probably the worst any child will ever experience. Its effects should never be under-estimated or ignored, even if many years have passed. Children may become fixated or emotionally frozen as a result of being separated, and the risk of breakdown in a permanent family placement is very high because their shallowness seems to invite rejection. After several placements such children begin to attract 'labels' which state that they are immature, superficial in relationships, indiscriminate in affection, self-centred and so on.

David Croft, you will have noticed from his life graph, had nine moves in seven years, and was just such an 'emotionally frozen' child. Children like David hardly ever feel able to talk in an adult way about themselves. They need to find other ways of 'talking' and we need to find other ways of talking to them. There are lots of different methods, but essentially they are all based on the sort of communication that children themselves favour: using play as a means of communication and a means of working out situations.

Communication through play

What follows is not about advanced techniques, but about suggestions of ways of communicating with children which we have used successfully. Anyone who has seen children being parents to their dolls and copying their parents' ways of talking will realise that this is a good way for us to get through to children. To do this makes demands on us as adults, because it requires us to shed our inhibitions. We must enter the world of the child whilst being sensitive to what the child might be saying and being ready to respond accordingly.

We have used these 'communication through play' techniques with children of from three to fifteen years old. As we have gained confidence in using them, we have introduced these techniques into our preparation of the life story book rather than at the end, and now we often use play before we start with the life story book.

Glove puppets

Having one glove puppet to speak for you and another for the child to speak through is a useful way to talk with children of all ages, but is particularly useful with younger children. No matter how good a relationship you have with a child, most find difficulty in revealing their inner world. They feel safer disclosing their intimate thoughts through puppets because of the distance the puppet seems to provide. Usually a two-way conversation can be started by your puppet asking the child's puppet questions.

The following is a conversation between a foster mother and Susan, a five year old girl who had recently experienced separation from her parents. They spoke to each other through Kermit the frog (the foster mother) and a penguin puppet (the little girl).

Kermit	*Do you like it with Auntie Jane and Uncle Jim?*
Penguin	*Sometimes.*
Kermit	*Where would you like to live?*
Penguin	*With my mummy and daddy.*
Kermit	*Oh, if I could not live with my mummy and daddy I would feel very sad.*
Penguin	*I feel sad because I cannot live with them.*
Kermit	*Why can't you live with your mummy and daddy?*
Penguin	*Because they are no longer friends and do not love each other.*

Shortly after this conversation, Susan, who had not cried since the separation two weeks before, started to cry because 'permission' to grieve had been given.

Play people

We have used this technique with young children from three upwards with outstanding success, but we have also used it with older children after having first overcome our own inhibitions. As we said earlier, you need to be able to relax to join in this activity!

You can buy a 'family' of play people at a toy shop. The set we use has been made with recognisable expressions, such as happiness, sadness, anger and so on. There are white, black and mixed-race play people.

36

Children who are reluctant to talk directly about how they feel are prepared to talk about how the play people 'feel'. The technique involves telling a story which is basically the child's life story as depicted in the life graph, but transferred to the play people. Telling the story for the first time, we usually just talk about concrete facts: 'This is the mummy and she had a baby girl.' Eventually the child is drawn into the play – which may carry through several sessions – and will start to attribute feelings to the play people which mirror her inner world.

Children who have been subjected to acts of violence will frequently work out these experiences again. One child hurled the father figure around the room. Another five year old, a girl, was confused because her elderly short term foster mother had cried when she was moved to an adoptive family. Six months later she was still puzzled, but refused to talk about the incident. With the play people we were able to tell her a story about the little girl who had to move from her 'Nan' who she loved and this 'Nan' cried. She said, 'When I moved from my Nan she cried and I wanted to cry too but I was afraid to.' From this she was helped to understand what had happened and given reassurance that her 'Nan' was safe and well.

The empty chair

Children will accumulate resentment against adults in their past who have either disappointed or rejected them. Occasionally these feelings can be detected, but usually they remain guarded and unresolved. One way to reach out and bring them into the open is the 'empty chair', a Gestalt therapy technique which we found in Claudia Jewett's *Adopting the Older Child*.

Place an empty chair in the centre of the room. Ask the child to imagine that a person with whom he or she has some unfinished business is seated on it. The empty chair helps the child to focus on anything that is left unfinished.

David was interested and curious when we presented him with the empty chair. But he claimed he was unable to think of a suitable occupant for it. 'How about your mother?' we prompted. David then walked purposefully up to the chair and demanded to know, 'Why did you leave me? I want to kick your head in.' With a nervous laugh, he half-heartedly attempted to retract the statement. 'Are you angry with your mother?' we asked. 'Yes I am,' he replied.

It is often possible to use such expressions of anger constructively by encouraging the child to take over the role of the person in the chair so as to experience how the other person feels.

David sat in the chair and imagined he was his mother, while we pretended to be David. 'Why did you leave me?' I asked. 'I left you because I was quarrelling with your dad and we couldn't live together any more,' came his reply.

Play people, from left to right:
'Wedgie' white family, 'Wedgie' black family, both from Galt; 'Little People' figures from Fisher-Price.

The telephone

A toy telephone can be used in a similar way to an empty chair. Your child can be encouraged to telephone a person from the past and have an imaginary conversation with that person. Frequently this is too direct, but can be made less threatening by holding a telephone conversation between either puppets or dolls.

Sarah had been received into care as a four year old because she had suffered persistent cruelty from her mother's co-habitee. She had been placed in a foster home, but this had broken down after six months. Four months after this breakdown, the following play with dolls and telephone took place. We made two sets of parents with dolls; the father in one set had an angry face. The dolls were not given names and were not identified as foster parents or natural parents.*

Me   *Look at this little girl* (doll). *She cannot live with her birth Mummy. Do you think she will ever take love and care from this forever Mummy and Daddy?*

Sarah   *No, she can only take love and care from her birth Mummy and that man who lives with her is no good.*

Me   *(Gently) I do not think he is.*

Sarah   *Well, he is.*
(Sarah then picked up the angry male doll and moved him away from the Mummy doll.)

Me   *Look what happens.* (I took the Mummy doll to the angry male doll and re-united them.)

Sarah   *But he had gone away.* (She picked up the angry male doll and threw it across the room.)

Me   *Now look what happens. The birth Mummy goes and gets him back.*

We enacted this several times with Sarah hurling the angry male doll away and me taking the Mummy doll to collect it. Sarah was getting exasperated and announced she was going to 'telephone that Mummy'. She was already familiar with the telephone because we had 'played' with it in the past.

Me   *What do they call that Mummy?*

Sarah   *Margaret* (the name of her birth mother). *Hello. I want to know why that little girl cannot live with you. Why don't you get rid of that man so this little girl can come and get love and care?*
(At this point Sarah held the telephone out, a look of consternation and disbelief on her face.)

Me   *What is the matter?*

Sarah   *She has put the phone down on me.*

A powerful urge to pick Sarah up and comfort her hurt almost overwhelmed me. With some effort of will I concentrated on the doll play.

Me   *Poor little girl, she is in such a whirl.* (I spun the little girl doll around.) *She doesn't know where to go. She can't get love from her birth Mummy and will not take it from these forever Mummy and Daddy.*

Sarah   *Yes, she is all empty inside.*

Sarah decided to telephone the little girl and advise her to go and live with the forever Mummy and Daddy because she could get love and care from them. I suggested to Sarah that we should tell her we understand why she wants to love her birth Mummy too.

Sarah   *Yes, I know. She can love her birth Mummy, but she cannot live with her because her Mummy does not want this man to go.*

Shortly after this Sarah moved in and eventually settled with a new family.

At no time was this play interpreted to Sarah. For instance, obviously we felt she was the little girl doll, but we never attempted to make this link for her. Violet Oaklander, in *Windows to our Children*, (Real People Press 1978) considers that 'the process of work with the child is a gentle, flowing one – an organic event.' The work for Sarah using the dolls and telephone helped her to understand events in her life and start the process of coming to terms with them in a way that was non-threatening. We feel that if we had faced her with direct questions about why her foster placement disrupted, nothing would have been forthcoming.

Role play

With older children, particularly adolescents, one can be more direct. We frequently role play situations by suggesting to the teenagers that we will be them and they be another actor in the scene. This means that they have to 'direct' and be the 'scriptwriter' too. This can be a revealing experience for all concerned.

We discuss role play further in the section about working with adolescents in groups, page 40.

---

*This study first appeared in an article in *Community Care* in December 1982.

37

For help and ideas with this section we are grateful to Beulah Mills, a specialist worker with Leeds Social Services, and Janis Blackburn, an ethnic minorities fostering officer in Sheffield. We would welcome comments from black foster parents, social workers and children who have experience of being black or of mixed parentage in a social work setting.

When you are talking to children about their family history, background and future, you will come across many misconceptions they have about themselves. You will find many opportunities to give them a more positive self-image as well as more information about themselves. For black and mixed-parentage children there is an extra dimension to their feelings about themselves – colour. Preparation for life story book work always needs to be handled with extreme care and honesty, especially when you are trying to put things into their true perspective, and possibly even more so when you are working with black and mixed-parentage children – *particularly if you are white.*

At the start, if you are white and are making a life story book with such a child, you should be familiar with the correct terminology to use when referring to black people, as incorrect usage of words may inhibit rather than help. Terms such as 'coloured' or 'half-caste' are offensive and should not be used. They deny the child's blackness and the fact that society perceives him or her as black.

If you are white you should recognise that for the child, talking to a white person about race and racism is a poor substitute for talking to a black person. You should therefore make every effort *to involve a black worker.* Through this helper many questions can be answered at first hand and a link will be provided with a person with whom the child may be able to identify. This can be particularly useful for children who have been in care for a great part of their lives and may have had little contact with black people, or for children who are living far removed from their culture.

In many areas, black children in care are in a con-siderable minority and white people are the dominant group. For self-protection or because they have few other models, these children identify with being white and tolerate racial jokes for obvious reasons. Black and mixed-race children who 'think' they are white or try to make themselves white (by scrubbing their skins, for example) are set for a very destructive phase in the future. We need, as with all our children, to help them towards a positive self-image and to give them a sense of self-esteem. We need to help them to realise that it is not their being black or of mixed parentage which is the problem, but other people's attitudes to it. However, we also need to keep this matter in perspective and recognise that it is only one of the areas of potential difficulty for them, and that other areas in their lives also need to be given importance.

White workers should try to work through and resolve their own fears and doubts and not underplay issues of race, racism and colour, for in doing so they are providing a greater disservice to children by protect-ing them from the realities of their lives.

What can you do?

Whatever your colour, if you are working with a black or mixed parentage child on a life story book, you need to recognise the ongoing need of that child to talk about race and colour when he or she wishes to. When talking about family life, give children pictures of both black and white families. Ask them to talk about the people in the pictures and ask which is like them. Use this as a starting point for discussion.

Ask the child to draw a picture of him or herself as they would like to look. If they present a picture other than of how they are, use this for discussion of different racial looks, talking about characteristics of black and white people and stressing individual worth above race, whether black or white.

All children need a sense of their cultural background as well as of their family background. Try to get hold of pictures, posters and books of the child's (or their family's) country of origin.* (Do this too for white children from other countires.) Include pictures of famous black people, especially British blacks – writers, politicians, musicians and sportsmen and women – in the collection of material. Stress the achievements of the child's community when the opportunity arises. You might read and let the child have copies of *West Indian World, Caribbean Times* or *Asian Times*, for example. Visit or write to black in-formation centres and youth clubs to see what help they can give you. Children may want to know about subjects such as Islam or Rastafarianism, about what kind of food their birth families would eat and about how they should look after their hair and skin. Help them to find out about all these things. If there are

---

*Colouring books like *Your Skin and Mine* by Paul Shower (published by A and C Black) are useful.

festivals in your area, such as a Caribbean carnival, take the child to them. In London, the Commonwealth Institute with its exhibits from all the countries of the Commonwealth is a marvellous resource.

If the child you are working with is going to a new family who is white, discuss the potential disadvantages of being black in a white family, as well as talking about all the hopes and fears you would talk about with any child.

Jane's story

Jane is of mixed parentage, with a West Indian father and an English mother. Her mother had had an unhappy home life and left home at an early age to go to Liverpool. There she met Jane's father. They had a happy relationship and their first baby, Jane's sister, was welcome and well cared for. The relationship began to break up and, when she found she was pregnant again, Jane's mother was unhappy. By the time Jane was born her father had all but disappeared and Jane's birth was an unwelcome event.

By the time she was four Jane was in care; her older sister stayed with their mother. An attempt was made to place Jane in a long-term foster home, but this did not work out. Her mother was still concerned about her, but did not feel that Jane could ever return to her. When Jane was eight years old, it was decided that a second attempt should be made to foster her. This time a life story book would be made before the placement. During the process of making the book, it became clear that Jane did not really believe that she had a father or that she was of mixed race.

Jane had said that she was not prepared to leave the children's home and she would go and hide if her social worker came to talk to her about fostering. She agreed,

however, to make a life story book because she wanted to know more about herself. By drawing her family tree, talking about her birth certificate and discussing the 'facts of life', Jane came to accept that she had a father and that he had a name and could be talked about.

The next stage was to get Jane to accept that her father was black and that she therefore had a foot in the black community as well as the white one. I offered to get maps, photographs and posters of the island where her father came from. Jane eventually accepted this offer and started to talk to the other children and staff about her father. She faced derision from the other children but so fascinated was she by discovering her 'other half' that it did not deter her.

Being half black and half white had bothered Jane for a long time, but she had never found an opportunity to talk about it. Now that she could talk about it with more confidence, she could easily identify where her father had come from and she could see from her birth certificate who both her parents were. Because of her concern for Jane, her mother had willingly given photographs of her before she came into care, although she had no photograph of Jane's father.

By the time the life story book was up to date and Jane had also been given the opportunity to discuss the breakdown of her previous fostering, she felt secure enough in her sense of identity to consider trying again. She was placed with a new family and felt happy talking to them about her natural parents, and saw this was accepted by them when she showed them her life story book. She was adopted by this new family a year later.

Jane needed knowledge about all her past, present and future, part of which was that she was black as well as white. It was an important part of all the things she needed to sort out.

Working with families

When more than one child of a family is in care, it is possible to do some of the work of making a life story book together. (But we invariably provide each child with his or her own life story book too.) We have found that working with a family in a group progresses faster than working in a one-to-one situation. The work will, of course, depend on the ages of the children in the family. With older children you might consider using a modified form of the group programme for adolescents, described in the next section.

Normally it will be the oldest child who will provide the link for the others from past to present. That child may be the family 'historian', assisting you in helping the other members of the family to understand what has happened in their past and what is happening in the present. In doing so, the older children are able to extend their own knowledge and understanding too, and can begin to explain how they understand things to their siblings. This can be less threatening than explaining them to someone outside the family.

With a family group, we might ask how the oldest child can explain to the siblings why they became separated from their family of origin. Marie, 14 years old and the eldest of four children, felt that she had been the cause because of her 'bad behaviour'. When she declared this it was a revelation to her to find out that a younger brother and sister felt they were the cause too. From there, they were helped to reach an understanding of their mother's mental illness. They understood that there were reasons why they were now living in a children's home and that there was no need to seek to blame anyone, or to take the blame upon themselves, because the causes were beyond their control.

Working with adolescents in groups

We have shown how working with children from the same family can help in the process of making life story books. Working with a group of children who are not related can also be successful.

Children over twelve who have been in care for many years become unwilling to talk about their past, confused about the present and have little sense of hope for the future. We have found that providing a setting in which children share their pasts, their feelings about the present and their hopes for the future with others who have experienced similar difficulties can be a help and a comfort. A group preparation can be a way of reducing the sense of isolation many children feel and a means of freeing them to share similar feelings with others.

Children in care often consider that their families are abnormal and it can be a revelation to them that their families are like many others. One group of five children discovered in their exploration that not only had none of them ever met their fathers, or had not done so for many years, but also that they all came from many-fathered families and all had half brothers and sisters. No amount of assurance from an adult could, we feel, have helped these children to place their families in context as 'normal' as much as talking and sharing with their peers had.

To help get over the natural reluctance to discuss the past, present and future, we have worked out a programme of meetings (eight core meetings and then a few follow-up meetings) which divide roughly into three stages.

The first stage is to help the young people to develop an awareness of themselves, to begin to express their inner thoughts and feelings, and to look at the range of options open to a child in care – of which fostering is but one. How making a life story book might help is introduced as a discussion topic about halfway through this stage and books are being made individually during the second stage.

40

'Bridging' work (see page 30), the third stage, which is done partially within the group, can start only when the possibility of return to the natural family or a move to a foster family is imminent. Sometimes we have enlisted the help of children who have made life story books and who have been successfully placed during this bridging stage. This greatly facilitates discussion about hopes and fears, as well as injecting an element of reality.

Forming and working with a group

The group should be carefully selected. It is a working group which can perhaps accommodate one disruptive member, but rarely more. All the children's foster parents or social workers or residential social

The aim of such a group is to provide an atmosphere in which the children can talk freely about their doubts and fears. Of course, the comments we have made earlier about confidentiality apply here too. Our major source of ideas about the content of such groups comes from Violet Oaklander's *Windows to our Children* (Real People Press 1978) and we suggest that you read this book as part of your preparation. We describe here the content of the group sessions, which, as with other ideas in this book, you may need to adapt for your own needs.

Depending on the time of year, and the time available, we have found it valuable to arrange a trip out early in the life of the group and additional to the normal sessions. This, we find, helps to form a group identity.

41

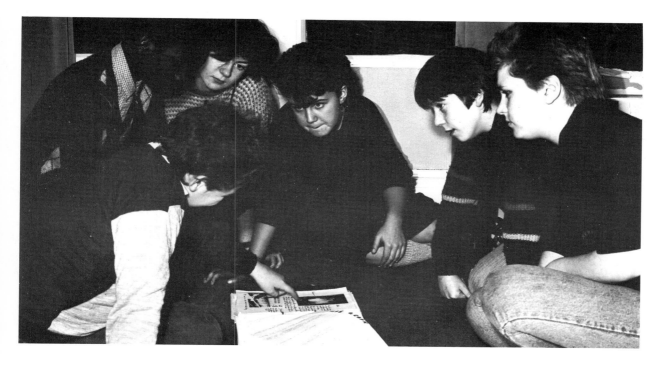

workers must have agreed in advance that they will make a life story book with their child and understand what they will be taking on in doing this. Meetings can be arranged with those involved with the child to explain the broad outline of what you are doing and to discuss the problems of possible regression.

Usually we work with six children and two to three leaders. The initial group-work runs for eight weekly sessions of about 1½ hours and includes the sharing of a simple meal. Planning and recording takes a further two hour meeting of the leaders each week. At session three the idea of a life story book is introduced.

A programme for group work

Session One

Before this first meeting each child will have been visited by one of the leaders and been given a personal explanation of what will be happening.

The session starts with a brief explanation of the aims and purposes of the group and an introduction of the group members. Then we start work with some 'warm up' exercises in which everyone is involved. For example, we sit in a circle and throw a ball between us, first calling out our own name and then throwing a ball to a group member and calling out their name, until the ball has passed to each person.

We use the game 'I went to market and bought some Apples.' The next person repeats this and adds a word beginning with the next letter of the alphabet. They might say, 'I went to market and bought some Apples and Bananas.' The next person might say, 'I went to market and bought some Apples, some Bananas and some Cauliflowers,' and so on through the alphabet.

We then move on to 'brainstorming' ideas. For this we have a flip chart mounted on an easel. The children call out ideas related to the topic under consideration and these are written down on the flip chart. If any child is prepared to do the writing we let them do so. Two or three topics can be covered in a session. The first brainstorm topic is 'Why are we here?' We use the contributions on the flip chart as a basis of discussion and soon we break for a simple meal, during which the discussion continues.

We then have a brainstorming session to create 'Feelings' cards like those discussed on page 20. The purpose of this activity is to introduce the concept of words to describe emotions. Ask the children to call out words that describe feelings, like sad, happy, angry and so on. Write these down on individual cards. Then the group, including the leaders, draw faces to match the feelings. Continue this game with individuals miming a 'feeling'.

The final brainstorming session is on 'What is a family?' The ideas of what constitutes a family are then used in the discussion. Remember at this stage not to force the pace of the group or try and lead it where it does not want to go.

Finish the session with some group game, perhaps 'I went to market' again.

Session Two

Open the session with the group's very own game, 'I went to market'. The group has to try and recall the correct sequence from the previous week. Return to the work on 'feelings' cards with further miming of the faces, and then asking the group to identify feelings that can be attributed to a face. Write these 'feelings' down on the cards.

The simple meal could take place at this point or after the first brainstorming session, as appropriate.

The brainstorm topic is 'Why do children come into care?' This could be threatening to members of the group and you may prefer to distance it for them by drawing either a boy or a girl on the flip chart, give it a name and title the session 'Why did Andrew (or Mary) come into care?' Use the material for discussion, gently moving the discussion towards how 'Andrew' might have felt. Encourage the use of the 'feelings' words introduced earlier.

What Violet Oaklander calls a 'fantasy trip' could follow. She suggests that relaxation exercises are useful before starting the work itself. We use several, for example:

Close your eyes. Starting with your toes, tense them. Gradually move up your body, tensing each muscle. Foot, leg, thigh and so on, right up to the head. Now let out all that tension slowly, feel it ebb away.

Then ask the group to close their eyes and take them on a fantasy trip. (This will lead to a drawing session, so have a supply of paper and colouring pencils ready.)

Let's pretend we're on an island. Take a walk through the island. Notice things: the colour of the flowers, the birds, the animals, fruit on the trees, the noises and smells. Suddenly, you enter a clearing and there is a big castle. Enter the courtyard. Walk across it. Enter the big hall. It is empty. You notice a staircase. Climb the stairs. At the top of the staircase there is a long corridor. You walk along it and you notice there are names on the doors. At the door with your name on it you stop. Enter the room. Have a good look round. Notice things. How does the room look? One last look around. Right, now open your eyes.

Now ask the group not to speak, but to draw a picture of what they saw in the room. The leaders can draw pictures too.

When the pictures are ready, a leader asks individuals to share their drawings with them. Let the children describe the picture in their own words. Do not be tempted to interpret the picture back. Instead, for example, if a child has drawn a settee, you might ask what the settee is either thinking or feeling. What is it saying? We usually write down on the drawing the child's comments, encouraging the use of 'feeling' words where this is appropriate.

Violet Oaklander believes that it is important to encourage children to share themselves. She regards it as a means of 'promoting the child's self discovery by asking him to elaborate on the parts of the picture. Making parts clearer, more obvious. Describing the shapes, forms, colours, representations, objects and people.'

You could finish off this session by playing a quiet game like 'sleeping lions'. Everyone stretches out on the floor and pretends to be a sleeping lion. One member, without physically touching anyone, attempts to get the others to move. He or she can pull faces, pretend to jump on a group member, blow on them, but must not touch anyone. Any movement or noise means that a person is no longer a sleeping lion and is therefore out of the game.

Session Three

Start with a group game, perhaps still 'I went to market'. Have a brainstorming session on *'What is a children's home?'* and follow this up with discussion. Go on to a brainstorming session on *'How did Andrew feel on his first day in care?'* and follow this with role playing about 'Andrew' coming into care with the children playing different roles. The meal break might follow this, with the discussion continuing.

Another of Violet Oaklander's fantasy trips could then be introduced.

Close your eyes. Imagine you are a rose. What kind of rosebush are you? Are you very small? Are you large? Are you fat? Are you tall? Do you have flowers? If so, what kind? What are your stems and branches like? What are your roots like? Do you have any roots? Do you have leaves? What kind? Do you have thorns? Where are you? In a yard? In a park? In the desert? In the city? In the country? In the middle of the ocean?
Are you in a pot, or growing in the ground, or through cement, or even inside somewhere? What's around you? Are there flowers or are you alone? Are there trees, animals, people, birds?
Do you look like a rosebush or something else? Is there anything around you? Like a fence? If so, what is it like? Or are you just in an open place?
What's it like to be a rose bush? How do you survive? Does someone take care of you?
What's the weather like for you right now?
*Open your eyes. Draw yourself as a rosebush.**

---

*This passage is quoted from Violet Oaklander's *Windows to our Children* (Real People Press, 1978).

Encourage the children to tell you about their drawings individually. Write on the drawing the thoughts and feelings of the rose bush. Do not be tempted to interpret the picture to the child.

Now is the time to introduce the idea of the life story book. Brainstorm the question *'What are life story books?'* first. One group's contributions to the flipchart were:

You read them
Birds and the bees
Biography
You write them
You enjoy them
I don't like them
You put photographs in them
Horrid
Feel bad if you don't talk about things

Use the material on the flipchart for discussion, acknowledging and accepting that making a life story book can be painful. Lead into how someone will be offering to make a life story book with each one of them. Finish this session with a quiet game.

Following this session, you should have a meeting with those who will be working individually on making a life story book with each child. The purpose is to share the broad outline of the group-work, to explain how you have been using the material, and for mutual support. This meeting is particularly important if the child is displaying signs of regression.

Session Four

Open with a simple game. The work can be more loosely structured from now on. Sometimes we bring in a box of 'play people' and glove puppets and wait for the children to take the lead. Frequently we have conversations between the dolls and puppets, talking about what they are thinking and feeling. This may lead to role playing from something either a doll or a puppet has been 'saying'.

For another group activity a leader has a large sheet of card on which he or she draws a shape, then might say and write, 'This is me, a red circle. I am all alone.' Someone else then draws a shape anywhere on the card, makes a comment and writes it down. (If we know that one of the group has difficulty with writing, one of the leaders takes responsibility for writing down all the comments.) The game continues until everyone has drawn at least two shapes.

43

Fit into the flow of the work any of these brainstorms: *'What is a family?' 'What is a children's home?' 'What is a foster family?'* It is sometimes useful to return to earlier brainstorm topics, like *'What is a children's home?'*. The group's perceptions will change with time.

Allow the children to express their feelings. If they make negative comments, do not try to persuade them differently. These topics usually raise fears about confidentiality. If so, reassure the group. You might lead on from this to a brainstorm on *'Who can you trust?'*.

44   If there is time during the session, we use Vera Fahlberg's three parents model (see page 33) to discuss how being in care changes natural parents' rights and responsibilities, to reassure the children that no one is trying to take away what they were endowed with at birth and to explain the position of the foster parents.

Session Five

Open with 'I went to market', followed by a group game, such as 'You've done it again, Mabel': the group stands in a circle with one member in the centre. Another players jumps into the circle and says, 'You've done it again, Mabel, you've (for example) not paid the rent for five weeks.' The first person can either respond to this by explaining why 'Mabel has done it again' or admit that this is so by rejoining the circle. If 'Mabel' goes out, the accuser becomes the new 'Mabel' and another player jumps into the circle adding another accusation, 'You've done it again, Mabel, you've . . .' and so the game continues, until everyone has had a turn or interest begins to wane. The group then breaks for its simple meal together.

Afterwards we use a poem recommended by Violet Oaklander. It was written by an eight year old girl and translated from the Turkish. Read it aloud while the group sits, eyes closed. (This poem can produce a powerful reaction, so you will have to try and gauge whether the group is ready for it.)

There is a Knot

There is a knot inside me
A knot which cannot be untied
Strong
It hurts
As if they had put a stone
Inside of me

I always remember the old days
Playing at our summer house
Going to grandmother's
Staying at grandmother's
I want those days to return
Perhaps the knot will be untied when they return
But there is a knot inside of me
So strong
And it hurts
*As if it is a stone inside of me**

The group then draws pictures and the leaders talk to each child about their picture.

One 13 year old girl wrote her own poem which we use too:**

I'd like to fly
I'd like to but I can't
I wasn't meant to
but I want to
I was meant to be me.
Why?
For some reason!
I wish I was a bird
to fly and be free
I feel I am imprisoned
In anyway I am what
I am nobody can change
that or make that
but I wish.

*Reproduced from *Have you Seen a Comet?*: Children's Art and Writing from Around the World (U.S. Committee for Unicef, New York and The John Day Company.)

**Reproduced by kind permission of Angie

You could suggest that they draw Andrew/Mary from session three with their knot inside them. This could lead to discussion of how Andrew/Mary might tell the others in the children's home how they feel inside.

By this stage in the life of the group you need to be sensitive to the issues the group might want to raise. For example, group members, especially if they are older children, might have experienced foster parent breakdowns and may want to talk about this.

One group brainstormed the advantages and disadvantages of being in a foster home:

Advantages	Disadvantages
Somewhere to go and live	Break down
Improves your life	Ruins your life
You like them	Waste of time
Better than your own	Using them
home	Isn't your own home

At the end of the session close with a quiet, relaxing game.

Session Six

Open with a game. It could be a 'scribble game' (from Violet Oaklander).

Everyone stands with space around them. They close their eyes and pretend to scribble on a giant sheet of paper. Then they are each given paper and pens and close their eyes and reproduce this scribble on their paper. When they open their eyes they try to identify the shapes produced.

From here they can go on to draw a picture of a time when they were laughed at. If this is too threatening, they can draw a time when Mary/Andrew were laughed at. Alternatively they can take another fantasy trip in which a boat in a storm is described while the group sit, eyes closed. Then the group draw what they saw. The simple meal can be taken together after this.

Move on to a group story. We have some cards with pictures of houses, cars, a cat, a dog, an eagle, items of clothing and so on. We put a picture on the table and say something about it. 'This is a house in a town.' The next person says something further about it, such as 'and the stick of dynamite came along to blow it up.' In one group someone put down a picture of a cat and added, 'Along came a lion and started to roar.' This was ridiculed by the group and used to discuss when we pretend about things.

You could then go on to brainstorm *'How can we find foster families?'*

In dealing with this subject with older children we try and help them understand how difficult it is to find substitute families for them. This can be discussed before the brainstorming session and it can be followed with a discussion about how to recruit substitute or foster families.

By this stage the children will be meeting their individual social workers and be making their life story books. We look at what they are doing and the ways that it might be of help in placement.

We might use role playing here:
Foster parents being interviewed
Andrew/Mary's first visit to a new foster family
A problem which might arise in a foster family, like Andrew caught smoking or Mary being accused of stealing
We stop the role play frequently in mid-stream and get the participants to change roles. We encourage them to talk about how it 'felt' in the role. We stop the role play and invite the group to say what a child's or foster parent's or social worker's secret voice might be saying inside them. If appropriate we use the candle technique (see page 32) to complement 'three parents' from the earlier session.

We close as usual with a relaxing game.

Session Seven

We use this session to illustrate how a life story book can be helpful by enlisting the help of an older child who has made a life story book and has been in placement for some time. This child needs to feel secure and you will have to spend time with him or her assisting with the preparation. Towards the end of the session the child's foster parents might be included in the discussion as well. If children have experienced a foster parent disruption, they often interrupt the session to talk about their experiences and make comparisons.

Thomas, whose story we told earlier on page 00, has spoken to groups about his life. When he reached the part of his story where he met his birth mother for the first time, it produced a barrage of questions: 'What was it like?' 'Did you cry?' 'Did she cry?' 'Did you kiss each other?' Thomas's reply stunned them. 'No, I didn't feel anything. It could have been someone in the street. I felt nothing.'

45

One child asked Thomas how he had expected his mother to be. 'Tall and rich,' was the wry reply. This, of course, vividly demonstrated how we all have fantasy pictures in our minds.

Frequently the group will use this session to talk about their feelings about their birth families. The group should close on a note of optimism as they understand how making a life story book to establish the past is helpful.

Session Eight

This is the final session of the first phase and needs to be organised around the feelings of loss that will be felt by all. Open by talking about the previous session. Ask members to draw something they remember from it and use their drawings for discussion.

Have the simple meal together, with perhaps a special treat to mark the occasion. Go on to brainstorm *'What was this group about? What should be included in the next group for other children?'* Follow with a quiet drawing session in which the members of the group might draw cards for each other. End with a brainstorm on *'How do we feel?'*

There should be at least two follow-up group meetings at six-weekly intervals. Before they go, remind the group of this and that they will be meeting together again.

Before the next meeting get together with the children's individual workers to talk about the progress they are making with the life story books and to discuss the broad features of the group.

Session Nine

This should be arranged about six weeks after the core group finishes. If substitute families have been found for some of the children, the focus can be orientated towards 'bridging' work. Whenever possible the leaders should have made contact at least once during the intervening six weeks. Send a letter about a week before the meeting to remind the child of the date, and suggest in it that they might like to bring along their life story book.

The session can be loosely structured around what you have done in earlier sessions. We find that many children are prepared to share their life story books with the group. This can lead to discussion of the feelings that making the books invoked.

Inevitably expectations will have been aroused about substitute families. With older children these may not be fulfilled. The group will need to look at the reality of this and be helped to talk about their disappointment and frustrations.

During the six-week interval before the next meeting, there will be further meetings with the children's individual social workers.

Session Ten

The purpose of this session is to reinforce the skills acquired through the group meetings: the ability of the children to talk about their hopes, fears and pain. The focus of this meeting will depend upon what has happened or is about to happen in their lives. If some children are now in placement, sharing their experiences might be usefully explored. We have used Parenting Plus material* to give children some insight into how moving into a foster family can affect them. We have concentrated on that part of the material which confronts foster parents with the changes they will have to make. Frequently children have not considered the fact that foster parents have to make adjustments too.

Ideally there should be further meetings at intervals as a means of helping the group to give mutual support to one another. Between these meetings there should be further discussion with the children's individual foster parents.

Parenting Plus is a basic training course for foster parents designed by the National Foster Care Association.

It is certainly possible to work with mentally handicapped children using life story book methods, and mental handicap in a child should not by itself dissuade you from considering starting a book with a child. The lack of intelligence in children is not nearly so important as their ability to cope with and benefit from what life throws at them. This is not to say that like every other facet of a child, intelligence does not need to be taken into account when considering how to work with a child.

The ability to express oneself through words and pictures is important if a child is to benefit from the life story book process. This need not be through the written word and, if the child has little facility in recording things in writing, you must be prepared to take over the responsibility of writing things down, remembering to take even greater care not to impose your version of events on the child.

We describe elsewhere ways apart from writing and drawing to help children express themselves, and you will probably need to make greater use of these methods. The lower the level of literacy in children, the more you will need to find inventive ways to help them to record their lives.

While methods need to be varied, the basic principles of life story book making will need to be adhered to in working with mentally handicapped children. You will need to reduce the life story book principles to basics and see if there are ways of achieving the ends by methods normally used in working with mentally-handicapped children.

The basics of this work we would consider to be:
communication
information giving
identity building
attention giving
All these factors are closely inter-related but still have identifiable strands.

Communicating is probably the most problematic issue with mentally handicapped children. Most communication needs to be pictorial and/or confined to easily understood words. At first a lot of communication will be one way, but it will eventually become more of a dialogue. You will always need extra sensitivity to discover when a mentally handicapped person is trying to establish communication with you.

Information giving is part of communication, naturally, and needs to be concise and basic. Photographs are particularly useful when you are working with someone who has little or no writing and whose ability to use abstract thought is limited. Repetition is esecially important and you need to do a resumé of all the previous session at the beginning of, and even during, each session. Sessions may need to be shorter to allow for a more limited concentration span.

The need for *identity building* is as important for the mentally handicapped person as it is for anyone else. You need again to be more sensitive than usual to see where the gaps are and to help to fill them.

Life story book work has the advantage of giving a child concentrated *attention* while doing work which has a recognised purpose and is therefore acceptable. Most children enjoy this and mentally handicapped children are no exception — by giving attention to a child you are saying 'you and your life are important'. For a child away from the natural family and facing the relative anonymity of being 'in care', this function of life story book work is very valuable.

Finally, you must be the judge of the depth of handicap with a particular child and whether you can work with him or her. The term 'mental handicap' covers a wide range of ability but in our experience work with such children is no more problematic than with children of average academic ability.•

47

• An excellent description of life story book work with a mentally handicapped child is in an unpublished dissertation by Roy Goddard, Coventry Social Services Department (193 Princethorpe Way, Ernsford Grange, Coventry CV3 2GB).

Further Reading

Rather than suggest many books from the vast number concerning children, we recommend here titles which have been a source of inspiration to us in our work, together with brief descriptions to help the reader decide what would be most useful.

Titles published by British Agencies for Adoption & Fostering (BAAF) are available from 11 Southwark Street, London SE1 1RQ (tel: 01-407 8800). The other titles are available through Bookstall Services, 86 Abbey Street, Derby, DE3 3SQ (tel: 0332 368039).

48

A General

Opening new doors by Kay Donley (BAAF 1975 and 1981). Based on talks given by the author, Director of the innovative 'Spaulding for Children' agency in the USA. In this book she challenges social workers to adopt new methods of finding families; sections are included on working with children, the mechanics of placement and post-placement services.

Attachment and separation (1981); *Helping children when they must move* (1981); *Child development* (1982); all by Vera Fahlberg and published by BAAF. Three useful workbooks containing text and exercises written by an American psychotherapist with a paediatric background.

Vera Fahlberg has also produced a film: *Adoptive children, adaptive feelings*, which is available on hire from Concord Films Council, 201 Felixstowe Road, Ipswich, Suffolk IP3 9BJ.

Adopting the older child by Claudia Jewett (Harvard Common Press, Harvard, Mass, USA, 1978) is another American book by a writer with considerable professional experience in placing older children in permanent families. She and her husband have three natural children and have adopted seven children too. This book, written in narrative style, tells the story of five children and the four families they are placed with. The index contains useful references to such topics as stealing, lying and school problems so that you can turn to these to see how the families dealt with them.

Windows to our children: a Gestalt therapy approach to children and adults by Violet Oaklander (Real People Press, Moab, Utah, USA, 1978) is jam-packed with ideas for working with children using many different approaches: drawing, fantasy trips, using clay, making things, reading and writing poetry, telling stories, using puppets, using sight, sound and touch. It also looks at ways of helping children with specific behaviour problems, such as aggressive behaviour, anger, bed-wetting and so on.

Dibs: in search of self by Virginia Axline (first published in the USA in 1964; now available in Pelican paperback from Penguin, 1971). A detailed, fascinating and very moving account of how an emotionally disturbed child was helped to find himself through play therapy.

Life Books for Children in Care (Northern Ireland Foster Care Association, 1984) gives examples of how life books have been used in different settings by different categories of child care workers.

B Articles in Community Care by Tony Ryan

From their point of view (12 November 1981)
A single parent, Mavis, and her adopted son, John, describe the difficulties they experienced in the early stages of placement.

"I'm lucky to have a Mum like Mavis and a real Mum and Gran like you" (21 July 1983)
Mavis and John describe how they visited John's eight previous placements. Both talk of how it felt to meet John's natural parents for the first time since he was left in hospital as a baby.

Telling it how it really is (25 February 1982)
A description of how the author first tackled a life story book. 'Bridging' is explained in the context of a case history.

Learning from failures (1 December 1982)
An account of how a child's substitute family placement disrupted because of her over investment in her past and the work preparation required before she was placed in a family again.

A problem filed (28 August 1983)
A personal account of reading a child's file which contained information about the time she had been fostered by the author.

BAAF

practice notes 12
information for adoptive parents
about their child's background

ISSN 0264-3111
July 1986

British Agencies for Adoption & Fostering
11 Southwark Street, London, SE1 1RQ

Telephone 01-407 8800

1. INTRODUCTION

1.1 Adoption workers have recognised for some time the importance of giving adoptive parents adequate information about the children to be placed with them and this has now been made mandatory as follows:

Regulation 12(1) of the Adoption Agencies Regulations 1983 states:

'Where an adoption agency has decided . . . that a prospective adopter would be a suitable adoptive parent for a particular child, it shall provide the prospective adopter with written information about the child, his personal history and background, including his religious and cultural background, his health history and current state of health . . .'

Regulation 20(1) of the Adoption Agencies (Scotland) Regulations 1984 states:

'Where an adoptive agency has decided . . . that a prospective adopter would be a suitable adoptive parent for a particular child it shall provide the person proposing to adopt the child with:

written information about the child's background, parentage, health and emotional developments.'

The wording may not be identical, but the import and intent is similar and this practice note applies to both sides of the border unless a specific exception is made.

1.2 Although children under one year old still make up a significant proportion of the total number of children adopted (21 per cent in Britain in 1984), they are no longer typical of adoption today. Children of all ages are now adopted. They come from a variety of backgrounds and from many different ethnic origins. Some of them are handicapped, and some have serious medical problems. There are also in-family adoptions by long-term foster parents, and sometimes adoptions are contested by natural parents. The principles described here, if used with flexibility and imagination, apply in all cases.

1.3 It is important to recognise how much can be covered in a short practice note. Unfortunately we cannot hope adequately to deal with the situation of childen in foster or residential care, but much of the content is highly relevant to these children too. The focus of this note is the provision of information to adopters. A further note is planned on information for adopted people.

1.4 The duty of adoption agencies to collect and pass on to adoptive parents (and thus to the child) information about the child's background is not matched by a corresponding duty of disclosure on the part of those who hold the information. Problems that will sometimes result from this situation can be reduced, but not eliminated, by good social work practice. We should like to emphasise the importance of working with natural parents and other relatives so that full information is given voluntarily and with understanding, but at the same time it must be remembered that we cannot compel them to disclose information.

When, after intensive work, consent is still refused, we believe that other professionals, eg doctors, psychologists and social workers, should be able to supply relevant information at the request of the adoption agency. We are concerned to protect the interests of the child in circumstances where child and parent are unable to remain together. We argue that once adults have given birth to children they bear a responsibility to make available the means to help their children to interpret their genetic inheritance. In the final analysis, we believe that a child's right and thus the adopters' need for crucial background information should outweigh the natural parents' rights to confidentiality in these matters. In law, however, the decision to disclose information held outside the agency remains with the holder of that information. The extent to which a doctor, for instance, can disclose information without the patient's consent may depend upon a court's interpretation of the degree of risk to the child if information is not disclosed. Until more cases are tested in court some doctors are likely to be reluctant to disclose even when they accept the principle of the child's right and need to know. It should be considered as a duty to encourage a parent to consent to disclosure.

2. ARGUMENTS FOR AND AGAINST DISCLOSURE OF INFORMATION

2.1 Why should full information be given to adoptive parents? We believe that the main purpose is to help them to be, in the fullest sense possible, loving and supportive parents to their adopted children. Information about background allows adoptive parents, like natural parents, to answer children's questions about origins, to discuss family likenesses and to respond to doctors' questions about family medical history. The role and the position of the adoptive parents is undermined if they constantly have to say 'I don't know'. Anyone's sense of identity is undermined if throughout life they are unable to answer questions about their genetic, social and cultural inheritance. There is ample evidence from adoption practice and research that children's well-being requires access to information about their roots.

2.2 Several counter-arguments have been put forward but can, we believe, be effectively answered:

"Natural families sometimes withhold information from their children."

The fact that this happens is no justification for adoption workers encouraging adoptive parents to do so. In non-adoptive families the child will probably have other sources of information, whereas the adopted child is often dependent on what the adoption agency has told the adoptive parents.

"Some information should be withheld because it is too distressing or sensitive."

We cannot assume that we know what other people will find easy or difficult to accept and information which seems highly sensitive to one person may be commonplace to another. In spite of the anxiety created for social workers, doctors and other professionals in giving distressing information to prospective adopters, there are very few situations in which the withholding of such information would be justified. Dramatic events like murder or other serious crimes are often public knowledge and may come to light in an unplanned way. Skeletons are notorious for not remaining in cupboards and children often know when subjects are being avoided. For adoptive parents too the truth about their child's background may be less distressing than uncertainty or fantasy.

We are not saying that other people in the adoptive family's social circle or chance acquaintances have a right to such information. On the contrary, we believe that adopters and later the children themselves can be helped to deal with everyday questions about their children's previous lives without recourse either to the whole truth or to a fragile web of invention.

"Some information, eg the possible degree of disability, can be given after the placement."

Prospective adopters need full information about the child and his or her background so that they can decide whether they can offer a permanent home. Although the adoption agency may keep in touch with the family after the court order, it has no right or duty to do so, and distance may discourage contact. Although good practice indicates that the agency should remain available for support, from the time of the court order the adoptive parents carry ultimate responsibility for their children. They need information in order to fulfil their role as parents.

"The disclosure of some information will infringe the rights of other people to confidentiality."

We have already stated in paragraph 1.4 our belief that the rights of the child and thus the adopters should outweigh those of the natural family in the case of relevant basic personal and medical information. When consent has not been given to the disclosure of information that is not essential to the child's well being, an alternative of partial but still useful information can often be found. An example of this is the use of first names and district rather than full names and addresses of former caretakers.

3. METHOD OF DISCLOSURE: ORAL OR WRITTEN?

3.1 The regulations refer only to written information and state that the information must be given after the agency decision and (in England and Wales) before the placement. The giving of information earlier or later as well is not precluded, and several stages of information giving is often advisable.

3.2 Once the agency identifies potential adopters for a child, *oral* information about the child and his or her background will help the prospective adopters decide if this is likely to be the child for them. At this explanatory stage it will also be advisable, especially if the child has any kind of disability, to refer the prospective adopters to written information on the disability and to encourage them to discuss the practical implications with a specialist and with parents of like children. This could also be the time for adopters to study any life story material with the child's social worker and to learn about the nature of the child's experiences.

The relevant medical information can be collected on the BAAF form NP (Medical Report on Mother/ Father of a child requiring adoption or long-term care). BAAF form E (Details of child needing placement) provides a format for collecting some of the other information required.

3.3 Written information about the child must be supplied once the placement decision has been made. This is an important stage; professional workers should make opportunities for full discussion with the adopters and should make sure that all the implications of the information are understood. If further oral information is supplied it should be confirmed in writing. Written information can be referred to whenever the need arises and is less subject to distortion through time. Any temptation to avoid writing down painful information should be resisted and where such information has to be conveyed, extra time should be allowed again for the exploration of implications and feelings.

3.4 Some adoptive parents find telling their children about their original family far from easy and all adopters should be encouraged to contact the agency for further discussion at any stage. Adopters should be helped to accept this continuing availability as part of an adoption service and should be assured that an approach would not be seen as a sign of failure.

4. CONTENT OF INFORMATION

4.1 *Principles*
Certain basic principles should guide the selection and presentation of information:

a) there should be complete honesty in all matters judged to be relevant, now or in the future, to the well-being of the child and his or her adoptive parents

b) where there is distressing information, it should be balanced, as far as possible, by positive information

c) on most issues the information should be verified fact and its reliability should be checked

d) where opinions or conjectures about important events in the child's life are the only information available, these should be given: most people prefer some information to none. However, sources should be identified and such material clearly distinguished from factual information.

If, exceptionally, any deviation from these principles is felt to be necessary, the agency case record should note this with the reason.

4.2 *Checklist*
For older children, other information will have been provided during earlier discussions about the child and some of it should be included here. The basic list of information should include:

a) the reasons why the child was placed for adoption

b) the reasons why the adopters were felt to be 'right' for the child

c) details of the child's birth (place, date, day of week, time of day and weight) and the names and addresses of all caregivers until placement with the adopters (so that the child can talk about and/or ask about earlier episodes in his or her life); the reasons for any moves should also be recorded

d) the child's medical history from birth, including immunisations, illnesses, accidents and visits to hospitals or clinics, with names and addresses. Any medical information should be compiled or checked by the agency medical adviser*

e) names and addresses of all nurseries, playgroups and schools attended and dates of attendance; names of key teachers should also be given if known

f) details of major or significant events, both happy and unhappy, in the child's life. Attention should be drawn to any related photographs, drawings, possessions, etc.

g) names, ages and brief descriptions (height, colouring, jobs, interests, geographical links) of the child's natural parents plus any family medical history which may be relevant to the child (if available, the latter will have been included in the medical adviser's report – see d) above)

h) details of other blood relatives. Careful consideration should be given in each case as to how much information can be properly given about other relatives. We think that there is a very strong case for the child (and for the young child this means the adoptive parents) knowing the names, ages and whereabouts of his or her own siblings. Adopted children will often ask about other members of their original family and there seems good reason for adoptive parents to know something about the appearance and interests of the child's grandparents and uncles and aunts. Negative information, unless it has some relevance to the child's health prospects, is probably inappropriate, but information about the achievements and skills of members of the original family is especially helpful. The possibility of the child tracing other relatives in later life must be accepted, in the same way as the possible tracing of natural parents. The attention of adoptive parents should be drawn to the delicacy of this issue, especially if there are much younger siblings placed elsewhere

i) any expressed wishes of the natural parents regarding future links with the child. Some may feel strongly that they want no further contact at any stage while others may welcome the offer of an occasional photograph or look forward to making contact, if the child so wishes, when he or she becomes an adult. Clearly, plans for adoption with access to any member of the original family would need to be clearly spelt out for the adopters. All this information, with details of any facilitating arrangements, should also be recorded on the agency file.

---

*BAAF form MH and the back page of form C or D will often be sufficient. The complete form C or D should be sent to the GP.

5. INFORMATION FOR THE CHILD

It is part of the parental task to decide how and when to discuss certain subjects with children. It seems important to observe this principle in adoption and therefore to give information to the parents for the child. However, there will be some circumstances when it will be appropriate for a social worker or other professional (with the knowledge and consent of the adopters) to offer written information directly to the child. Obviously the style will be adjusted to the child's age and understanding.

6. INFORMATION WHICH EMERGES AFTER ADOPTION

Occasionally important information about the child's natural family comes to light some time after the adoption. The most likely events are the discovery of an hereditary condition in a member of the natural family or new information about a natural parent. In such circumstances the adoption team should decide on the best course of action in the light of all the available information.**

7. PRACTICALITIES

7.1 Although there is obviously an important area of overlap between the collection of information described in this practice note and work on a life story book, the two are not identical. It is important to remember that the life story belongs to the child and that it is not a substitute for full information compiled for adoptive parents.

7.2 The difficulties about collecting medical information on natural families may lessen in time but they will not disappear completely. Agencies should enlist the help of their medical advisers in explaining to medical colleagues the importance of obtaining this information. We hope that this practice note will also stimulate discussion of the issue in the Medical Defence Societies and in the medical profession as a whole.

See Medical Notes *Adoption & Fostering* **6 3 1982 for note on genetic counselling after adoption.

BAAF PRACTICE NOTES

1. *Private placements*
2. *Adoption and fostering panels*
3. *Consent for medical treatment for children in care or placed for adoption*
4. *Adoption panels in England and Wales*
5. *Medical aspects of the Adoption Agencies Regulations 1983 (England and Wales)*
6. *A-Z of changes in the law (England and Wales)*
7. *Using the media*
8. *A-Z of changes in the law (Scotland)*
9. *Medical aspects of the Adoption Agencies (Scotland) Regulations 1984*
10. *Using the BAAF medical forms*
11. *Custodianship*

© BAAF 1986